The Big Zero

The Big Zero

The Transformation of ZBB into a Force for Growth, Innovation and Competitive Advantage

KRIS TIMMERMANS, CHRIS ROARK AND RODRIGO ABDALLA

BUSINESS

PENGUIN BUSINESS

UK | USA | Canada | Ireland | Australia
India | New Zealand | South Africa

Penguin Business is part of the Penguin Random House group of companies
whose addresses can be found at global.penguinrandomhouse.com.

First published 2019

001

Copyright © Accenture Strategy, 2019

The moral right of the copyright holders has been asserted

Set in 12/14.75 pt Dante MT Std
Typeset by Jouve (UK), Milton Keynes
Printed and bound in Great Britain by Clays Ltd, Elcograf S.p.A.

A CIP catalogue record for this book is available from the British Library

ISBN: 978–0–241–40159–0

Contents

Introduction: A Rock and a Hard Place

Growth. It's what every company – from scrappy start-up to lumbering incumbent – strives for. But it's becoming more and more elusive as companies struggle to survive between a competitive rock and a hard place: keeping the core business humming on one side while transitioning to new business models and dedicating resources to stoke the engines of future growth on the other.

Yet an overwhelming majority (84 per cent) of business leaders are confident they will achieve their next three years' projected growth rates. A full 79 per cent think their organizations will grow revenue by 5 per cent or more.[1] While growth targets remain ambitious, the ability to achieve them is elusive at best. Consider this: the average GDP growth for OECD economies barely exceeds 3 per cent.[2]

Clearly, most of those business leaders will fall considerably short of their projections, primarily because it costs dearly to nurture new sources of growth. New channels, new systems, new capabilities, new resources, new skills – companies can't solve the problem of funding 'the new' through stopgap measures like borrowing more. Credit ratings bottom out. Expectations of profit margins only increase. Reducing dividends hurts market valuations. Brute force slash-and-burn cuts can effectively gut a business.

The most accessible source of funding involves taking out bad costs and optimizing good costs to help grow the core business and support the essential rotation to the new. The problem: costs creep back over time. A mere 36 per cent of executives believe their current cost reduction efforts are durable.[3] As a result, costs ride an oscillating curve: they creep up, there's a tactical intervention to bring them down, and over time they rise again when the effects of the cost reduction measure ebb away. And the cycle repeats into perpetuity, leaving companies in an endless state of reactively fending off cost bloat.

To break that cycle, there's a move in business today that calls for nothing less than a fundamental reshifting of resources to fund innovation and profitability. We call it 'ZBx', or 'zero-based mindset'. ZBx creates a culture of innovation, allowing companies to achieve start-up speed at enterprise scale. It's an approach that companies across all industries are undertaking to channel savings into new sources of growth and innovation.

'ZBx creates a culture of innovation, allowing companies to achieve start-up speed at enterprise scale.'

ZBx focuses on agility over austerity, visibility over guesswork, and the future over the past, to fuel growth and competitiveness. Creating a zero-based mindset isn't easy. This is about more than line items and balance sheets. It's about transforming a culture right down to its foundations by aligning the strategic priorities of the entire organization and reinvigorating people's mindsets and behaviours, endowing them with the ownership of what and how they spend and where they redeploy the savings.

With its focus on fostering forensic profit-and-loss transparency, a zero-based mindset gives decision makers a clear view of organizational structure, systems, financials and people. This, in turn, highlights those tasks, outlays, processes, reports (and potentially roles and organization units) that add little or no value. And these inefficient costs can be redeployed where they'll offer better return on investment. In essence, it drives a shift of inefficient 'bad costs' to efficient 'good costs' that will promote growth and create a distinct employee value proposition.

A zero-based mindset enables more accurate and quicker decisions to be made about market positioning and possible divestitures, acquisitions or internal restructuring, all of which can make the company more competitive. In other words, it provides a platform for agility that enables a company to move with confidence to transform the business. According to the latest research on competitive agility, boosting competitiveness means executing well across the interdependent areas of growth, profitability, sustainability and trust.[4] Companies with this multi-dimensional strategy are winners in improving all areas of agility.[5]

Take Unilever as an example. The company plans to save up to €2 billion using a zero-based mentality.[6,7] The Anglo-Dutch consumer giant strives to extend its use of zero-based budgeting to reduce spending in its marketing and logistics departments.[8] In addition, the company's 'Sustainable Living Plan' is geared at reducing Unilever's environmental footprint and doubling sales and long-term profitability by cutting non-working money and directing it toward business models with sustainability at their core.[9] The company is accelerating growth in core categories and geographic markets through more focused investments in innovation and marketing.

Unilever is just one of a multitude of companies in virtually every industry applying zero-based strategies to fuel greater competitive agility. We'll explore several other examples throughout this book.

About this book

How did zero-based budgeting evolve into the zero-based mindset and why? Which companies are using it to their advantage and how? And, most importantly, what are the capabilities needed for durable results? Throughout this book, we set out to help companies find their own path toward a successful zero-based mindset journey, moving from the highest-level perspective on zero-based budgeting's evolution to zero-based mindset and its impact on the organization's culture in Part I of the book to a review of the required capabilities in Part II.

The zero-based mindset is a response from the market for more holistic, sustainable corporate strategies, imbuing organizations with the ability to free up and reallocate funds for growth strategies essential to success. Organizations that start on the road to a zero-based mindset now are investing for the long haul, employing the latest in digital technology to shift cost curves down dramatically and reimagine work itself. Those that wait risk being wiped off the competitive map.

PART I

1. The (R)evolution of ZBx

There's a revolution afoot in the business world. One that's apparent by the sheer number of brands leading the charge: Anheuser-Busch InBev (AB InBev),[1] Coca-Cola,[2] ConAgra Foods,[3] Diageo,[4] Unilever[5] and Walmart,[6] to name a few standouts on an ever-growing list.[7] The zero-based mindset, or ZBx, is making these companies more agile by reinvesting in growth-oriented action.

But before we look at the revolution, it's helpful to understand ZBx's evolution in the private sector from zero-based budgeting (ZBB.) In 1970, a controller at Texas Instruments, Peter Pyhrr, codified what he called, 'zero-based budgeting' in an article published that year in the *Harvard Business Review*.[8] Pyhrr's idea was simple: instead of basing budgets on past years, the controller's approach was to start from scratch. At zero. In those early days, ZBB focused solely on administrative costs such as travel, office supplies and the like.[9]

In 1973 Jimmy Carter, then governor of Georgia, hired Pyhrr to roll out ZBB at the state level. And when he campaigned for president, Carter's promise to the American people was a balanced federal budget based partly on its tenets. When Ronald Reagan took office in 1981, he rolled back much of Carter's efforts and ZBB went into a dormant period.

Back in the private sector, zero-basing found three champions in the form of Jorge Paulo Lemann, Marcel Telles and Carlos Alberto Sicupira, a trio of friends who owned Garantia, an investment bank in Brazil.[10] In 1989 they bought Brahma, a local brewery, and used it as an acquisition vehicle that would culminate in the formation of AB InBev.[11] Through each successive move, the 'three men from Garantia' (or 3G Capital, as they would later be known) created and honed zero-based approaches in acquisitions of iconic brands including Burger King, Anheuser-Busch and Tim Horton's. In response to the threat of being acquired by 3G, hundreds of consumer-products companies launched similar zero-based initiatives.[12] At this point, ZBB had already evolved into a more sophisticated management tool. The only barrier to success was lack of ambition, not cultural issues.

This new version of ZBB borrowed from other approaches for cost reduction, planning and monitoring. The most notable of these was the concept of cost category ownership. Category ownership creates a healthy organizational tension between category and entity owners, fostering accountability, collaboration and shared budgetary goals.

After the millennium, ZBB underwent another evolutionary step change to become a full-fledged management technique that excises bad – non-working – costs while boosting good – working – costs. This ability became durable with the introduction of the closed-loop approach. Just like it sounds, closed-loop cost management is about making sure cut costs stay that way over time. It's a capability that involves gaining full visibility on all operating spend – across business units, categories and geographies – to a detailed level, and exploring how money can be spent more wisely to add value and drive growth. And it doesn't stop there. A virtuous cycle of control and monitoring that feeds back into forensic visibility ensures the longevity of efficiency and efficacy improvements.

But it wasn't until the present decade that organizations began to expand the concept into a broader-based approach to include other areas of the organization beyond administration. In 2016 Accenture spawned a progeny of 'baby Zs' that continue to create a buzz in boardrooms across industries: ZBS (zero-based spend), ZBO (zero-based organization), ZBC (zero-based commercial) and ZBSC (zero-based supply chain). This is when zero-based budgeting morphed into the all-encompassing zero-based mindset, or ZBx.

Research indicates that zero-based mindset programmes reduce costs sustainably by an average of 15 per cent and generate savings of more than $1 billion for scores of companies among the Global

2000.[13] These reductions can vary from 5 per cent to 28 per cent, depending on the level of ambition around the should-cost targets companies set for themselves.

So far, so good. But today we're in the age of an even more advanced ZBx. One underpinned by automation and digital tools radically shifting cost curves. It's no longer good enough to chase after incremental savings based on cutting or trimming line items. Today's ZBx is about reimagining what processes *should* cost, aiming for something we call 'quartile zero'.

What exactly do we mean by quartile zero? For years, companies followed a comparative approach to benchmarking cost reductions. They'd look to move from the highest quartile (i.e. worst-performing) in spend to the lowest, or 'quartile one', ultimately landing among those peer companies with 'best in class' spend. The focus was on identifying where the company outspent the leaders and how to shave costs to bring them in line with those setting the bar. The problem: this approach not only fails to fuel true competitive advantage, but also isn't aggressive enough because it looks only at traditional pricing and consumption patterns.[14] The more aggressive the aim for quartile zero, the more dramatic the savings.

'Today we're in the age of an even more advanced ZBx. One underpinned by automation and digital tools radically shifting cost curves. It's no longer good enough to chase after incremental savings based on cutting or trimming line items.'

Consider, for instance, spending on legal services. A company in the midst of an acquisition will have myriad contracts for review, adjustment, and ultimate approval – equating to hundreds of hours of time billed by the company's legal advisers. A traditional approach to reducing contract review costs would be to better control either price (negotiating a lower rate from the law firm) or consumption (agreeing to pay for fewer hours).

But what if the company uses artificial intelligence (AI) to handle much of the contract reviews? An AI solution can cut the amount of time lawyers spend on contract analysis by as much as 80 per cent. By using AI instead of just focusing on the traditional price or consumption levers, the company can drive down the total cost of contract reviews far more significantly – and set a new benchmark for what contract reviews should cost instead of what they cost now.

Plant maintenance is another area where quartile zero is impacting performance. Digital gives near real-time monitoring on things like gas compressors and turbines in oil refineries. Data is fed into control systems and into the hands of operations teams who can intervene at critical points, like when corrosion threatens to inhibit a machine's performance. AI allows companies to go from being reactive to proactive – anticipating problems before they disrupt service. After all, an average oil refinery shutting down for a day can cost upward of a million dollars.

The next frontier in ZBx is integrating humans and machines, so that machines can do what they do best: performing repetitive tasks, analysing huge data sets and handling routine activities. And humans can do what they do best: resolving ambiguous information, exercising judgement in difficult cases and dealing with dissatisfied customers. This integration will amplify human skills and help us achieve productivity gains previously unimaginable. This emerging symbiosis between man and machine is unlocking a new wave of business transformation.[15]

From Bee Gees to Beyoncé and beyond

Zero-based approaches have evolved from their disco days. Moving from a strict focus on cost cutting in SG&A to a holistic transformation that drives sustainable advantage across the organization. Helping companies get their competitive groove on and keep it for ever. Now that we've taken a look at zero-based approaches since the days of the Bee Gees, we'll delve into how it stands today, and explore how it reshifts resources to fund innovation and profitability.

2. The 'X' Factor

To meet the dizzying speed of change, companies are making strategic decisions from the highest levels of the organization about their future growth and direction, and reallocating resources to fund them. Organization-wide – not only in SG&A. Which means zero-basing everything with a lens on revenue and should-costs – from plant maintenance to marketing, sales and pricing strategies. The freed-up cash can then be reinvested to maximize output from the core while simultaneously identifying and funding new sources of growth.

It's an approach that calls for action in four areas: zero-based spend (ZBS), zero-based organization (ZBO), zero-based commercial (ZBC) and zero-based supply chain (ZBSC).

Getting granular through zero-based spend (ZBS)

General and administrative costs (G&A) are, of course, a vital part of any business. They keep the lights on, the systems operational, the business insured and a host of other activities running. But because they represent overhead, they can become a threat to the bottom line. They span virtually the entire enterprise and can eat up precious margin if not controlled – especially during times of rapid growth when it's easy to overlook G&A costs rising faster than sales. The plain fact is, to stay competitive, companies need to keep their G&A costs as low as possible over time.

ZBS is about identifying G&A with an unprecedented level of granularity. This allows leadership to make the right choices to change the culture of the organization, ultimately freeing up cash that can funnel into growth initiatives.

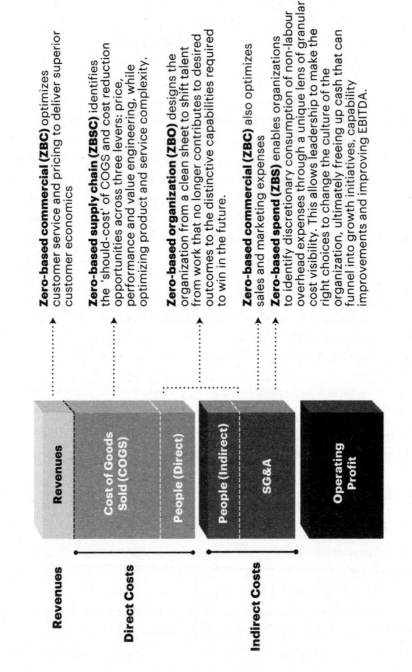

Zero-based commercial (ZBC) optimizes customer service and pricing to deliver superior customer economics

Zero-based supply chain (ZBSC) identifies the 'should-cost' of COGS and cost reduction opportunities across three levers: price, performance and value engineering, while optimizing product and service complexity.

Zero-based organization (ZBO) designs the organization from a clean sheet to shift talent from work that no longer contributes to desired outcomes to the distinctive capabilities required to win in the future.

Zero-based commercial (ZBC) also optimizes sales and marketing expenses

Zero-based spend (ZBS) enables organizations to identify discretionary consumption of non-labour overhead expenses through a unique lens of granular cost visibility. This allows leadership to make the right choices to change the culture of the organization, ultimately freeing up cash that can funnel into growth initiatives, capability improvements and improving EBITDA.

Revenues

Direct Costs

Indirect Costs

Revenues

Cost of Goods Sold (COGS)

People (Direct)

People (Indirect)

SG&A

Operating Profit

That doesn't mean implementing across-the-board cuts. A blanket edict to slash G&A budgets by X per cent can, in fact, harm a business. Such an approach fails to recognize the difference between the activities or functions that add value and those that don't (or those that may even destroy value). Good costs enhance a company's value proposition not only to customers but also to employees. For example, cutting 'extras' like in-office celebrations or other rewards can tarnish employee branding.

Companies need to gain true, ongoing visibility of their entire G&A spending to determine what they can reduce, and how the savings should be reallocated or reinvested – for example to fuel a digital transformation, enter new markets, or fund acquisitions. In short, ZBS can help companies get a handle on G&A costs strategically while unlocking resources that can be reallocated to revenue-generating activities.

Companies that run ZBS outperform their peers on average in EBITDA (an increase of 50 per cent versus 38 per cent) and revenues (growth of 28 per cent versus 22 per cent).[1] These companies also tend to exercise stronger financial discipline throughout their operations.

ZBS CASE STUDY

ZBS has helped drive the expansion of a leading telecoms company serving Africa and the Middle East. Faced with rising competition and declining margins in its core business, the company used ZBS to reset its operating budgets. Within six months it realized a $550 million annual cost reduction, including $250 million from new SG&A initiatives. Ultimately, improved margins helped the company step up its investments in areas of strategic importance and fueled growth initiatives.[2]

Kicking the tyres with zero-based organization (ZBO)

Serious soul searching is a prerequisite for designing an organization from a clean sheet. ZBO challenges a company's strategic ambition, choices and distinctive capabilities without the bias of the past. Think of it as kicking the tyres on what a company will and will not do, as well as what it will do differently. Staying relevant means developing a growth strategy and quickly realigning to a more agile organization to support it.

But while 82 per cent of companies are focused on freeing up funds to invest in growth initiatives,[3] only a quarter of executives believe their company's operating model has evolved quickly enough to align to their strategy.[4] So it's not enough to focus on cost-cutting. In parallel, companies need to change operating models to serve the demands of their future strategies.

This means working simultaneously on two fronts to drive competitive advantage and growth: 'getting brilliant at the basics' with process excellence and more efficient execution of core functions. And 'cutting new ground' to drive innovation, build distinctive capabilities and engage customers in wholly new ways.

ZBO CASE STUDY

Consider one global company in the consumer health-care industry. After undertaking a ZBO analysis, the company realized that the lion's share of its funding for sales and marketing was being funnelled to its most established markets because its year-on-year adjustments were based on the budget from the previous year. Up-and-coming markets were undernourished, and, as a result, not receiving the sales and marketing funding and

---

resources required to meet the company's hyper-growth ambition. ZBO helped in grouping markets differently, using complexity factors to create visibility and to re-direct resources appropriately. By redistributing savings from established markets to emerging ones, the company was able to deliver overall savings while reinvesting in growth markets.

Zero-based commercial (ZBC): seeing the whole

There's a famous quote from nineteenth-century US retailer John Wanamaker that goes: 'Half the money I spend on advertising is wasted; the trouble is, I don't know which half.'

It's fairly easy to calculate the profitability of products and business units. But ask most executives which customers are destroying the bottom line, and by how much, and you may hear the sound of silence. What's more, companies often lack the capability to differentiate between strategically important and transactional customers. This goes beyond traditional customer segmentation. It involves linking the type of customer relationship to the means and measures that drive enterprise profitability. In a cost-conscious, growth-focused environment, high-value customers – those that are profitable and strategic – should be the priority. If only companies could understand who they are and what matters most to the execution of the enterprise's growth strategy.

'Zero based budgeting is improving our productivity in brand and marketing investment as we reduce the cost of advertising production and increase investment in media channels. ZBB is also eliminating waste in those areas where we have over-saturated traditional media channels, as well as reducing overheads.'

– UNILEVER[5]

Businesses that have cracked this code have used zero-based commercial (ZBC) to build an actionable and sustainable customer economics model. This model enables the enterprise to define the right customer experiences and price points for each profit segment and evaluates total share of wallet to optimize commercial customer investments in a way that does not negatively impact revenue.

How does the ZBC customer economics approach work? Companies establish a P&L (profit and loss) for each customer, calculating the total cost-to-serve based on acquisition, sales force coverage, customer service, billing and shipping costs, among others. They then stratify the profitability of the entire customer base.

It's an eye-opening exercise. Executives are often surprised to discover the degree to which a small number of highly unprofitable customers can drag down an entire company's economics, or the dilutive impact that large-volume, low-margin customers can have on profitability. Insights like these are invaluable because they help reshape the customer portfolio to improve profitability and rebalance customer experiences to align with value.

Achieving game-changing results from ZBC requires strategic fundamentals of 'where to play' and 'how to win' to be addressed with rigour and granularity. Too often, organizations proceed directly to spend-optimization exercises that tend to focus more on procurement and less on how resources are strategically deployed across the set of customer-facing activities.

To be fair, the underlying reason is in part because today's customer journey has never been more daunting or complex. Analysis of traditional dimensions of customer, channel and product mix no longer provide adequate insight. Even relatively sophisticated marketing-mix models can miss the true return of specific activities, especially if they fail to consider upstream and downstream dynamics and customer and product life-stage and maturity.

Zero-based supply chain (ZBSC): ending the cost-reduction death spiral

Most manufacturing companies have a greater number of supply-chain initiatives on their agendas than they have resources to work on them. Yet they still try to tackle complex, systemic, long-standing issues with piecemeal continuous improvement programmes. In the process, they fail to build a clear picture of who's spending what and where. They continue to work in functional silos and move at a snail's pace to integrate the latest digital technology. And they limit sustainability initiatives to what's on their near-term horizons. Satisfied with small shifts in performance, companies significantly underestimate what disruption is doing to their future should-costs. In the process, they erode an already precarious cost position and make themselves ever more vulnerable to nimble competitors. Consequently, they become trapped in a supply chain cost-reduction death spiral.[6]

To accelerate the change and identify all unnecessary costs, ZBSC uses three levers: price, performance and value engineering, focusing on long-term sustainable cost reductions. Once global visibility of costs and performance for each facility is established, individual future target COGS can be set for each of them.

By combining the global view and local deep dives, consumption and price reduction opportunities can be identified for each plant. While the price opportunities are driven by applying sourcing levers, consumption is reduced by identifying and spreading local manufacturing and logistics best practices and value engineering ideas.

These initiatives cover every aspect of the supply chain, from turning by-products into a source of extra revenue, through reducing the amount of finished goods damaged in handling and transportation, all the way to analysing the physical footprint of plants and distribution centres and identifying consolidation opportunities. By continually improving results, ZBSC offers a coveted competitive advantage: the ability to capture supply-chain value in a rapidly changing world.

ZBSC CASE STUDY

A zero-based supply chain approach helped a global products company under continual major cost pressure to reset its baseline yearly. The company expanded existing zero-based principles to COGS, with an initial focus on logistics. It broke down barriers across business units and regions for granular visibility into cost and operational performance across transport and warehouse operations. A quartile-zero vision applying advanced analytics and technology impact across the supply chain – including automation for picking and packing and warehousing, and predictive analytics for optimizing movement and modes of raw materials and finished product – helped the company reset targets. The organization has identified more than 20 per cent cost reduction opportunity across the network and captured 12 per cent in the first twelve months.[7]

A note on zero-based projects

The majority of costs may reside in projects for some companies. That's why more and more organizations are applying the principles of ZBx to them as well. Why? Because a zero-based mindset can be applied to every aspect of project management, from strategic prioritization, governance and scoping, all the way to control and monitoring. Ultimately, the wider the use, the more value the zero-based mindset unearths. We haven't included a section dedicated to projects in this book, but the principles we examine are applicable to a broad range of initiatives in a wide variety of settings, including companies in project mode.

The 'X' factor in industries

How are different industries applying ZBx as part of their business strategy? And what are some of the outcomes and challenges experienced across these different sectors? Telecoms is just one of the many industries boosting agility and competitiveness by adopting a zero-based mindset. Within this hotbed of innovation, communications service providers (CSPs) are facing increasing pressure from new technologies and digital upstarts.

As a result, they are looking for ways to free up funds and adapt to market shifts to compete with often smaller, more nimble challengers, and new mega-competitors formed through mergers and acquisitions. To put things in perspective, a recent study found that traditional cost-reduction strategies can achieve only 35 per cent of the savings that the top fifty CSPs need to ensure ongoing category leadership.[8]

Leaders in every industry are using ZBx to become more resilient and innovative. In the oil and gas space, companies are turning to ZBx to scale quickly, given the need to weather pricing downturns and exploit periods of sudden growth. In the health-care industry, providers are capitalizing on ZBx to deliver more cost-effective and convenient services to patients. And leading manufacturers, retailers and distributors are leveraging ZBx to better manage demand and supply-chain operations.

Part of the key to their successful transformation is leveraging shifting cost curves. New technologies in the areas of AI and automation have impacted costs – reducing them precipitously as well as creating new opportunities for establishing what costs 'should be'. We'll look at that in the next chapter.

3. Zeroing in on Cost Curves

There's an emerging symbiosis between man and machine that is unlocking a third wave of business transformation and reconstituting what's possible through ZBx.[1] While the first wave involved standardized processes and the second consisted of automated processes, this third wave involves adaptive processes that are reimagined from scratch: moving them to the quartile-zero approach we mentioned in Chapter 1.

This third wave, driven by AI, has created a dynamic space in which humans and machines collaborate to attain orders-of-magnitude improvements in business performance. Humans work with smart machines to exploit what each party does best. Although many companies are piloting AI, only a small number of companies have started to transform how work is performed.

These applications are transformational and typically require human participation to apply expertise that is difficult to explain or model. Think of a bank's anti-money-laundering systems. A complicated financial transaction is processed, and an automated system flags it as suspicious. Humans decide whether it warrants further investigation, and the machine learns from that decision to adjust and improve the original algorithm.

In essence, machines are doing what they do best: performing repetitive tasks, analysing huge data sets and handling routine activities. And humans can do what they do best: resolving ambiguous information, exercising judgement in difficult cases and dealing with dissatisfied customers. They amplify each other's strengths, giving human workers superpowers. And in the process, companies achieve productivity gains that were previously inconceivable.

Businesses need to shift from seeing processes as a collection of nodes along a straight line. With quartile zero, processes can be viewed as a sprawling network of movable, reconnectable nodes or perhaps something with a hub and spokes. Either way, the linear model for processes no longer cuts it. The goal here is the fusion of humans and machines.

Quartile zero and the 'should-cost' mindset

Let's dive deeper into quartile zero. In benchmarking terms, you'll have heard of quartile three, quartile two and quartile one. For years, companies have followed a traditional benchmarking or comparative approach to cost reduction. They make improvements to key performance indicators (KPIs) in the highest quartile (i.e. the worst-performing) based on leading rivals. The problem is, this approach not only undermines true competitive advantage, because performance can only be as good as the best-in-class, but also isn't aggressive enough. Why? Because it doesn't exhaust the efficiency opportunity or thinking about the most strategic allocation of resources for the enterprise.

Quartile zero is a dramatic shift away from old-school comparative approaches. Rather than relying on first-quartile benchmarks, quartile zero starts with a clean sheet – true zero. From there, it considers how digital technologies, sustainability practices and other dynamic forces can redefine what a company's operations should cost, spurring a fundamental change in the cost curve. The impact of quartile-zero thinking is dramatic because digital technologies empower companies to far surpass even their best past performance and first-quartile benchmarks.[2]

The adaptive nature of AI-age processes is driven by real-time data rather than by an a priori sequence of steps. The paradox is that although these processes are not standardized or routine, they can repeatedly deliver excellent results. In fact, leading organizations have been able to bring to market individualized products and services (as opposed to the mass-produced goods of the past) and deliver profitable outcomes.[3]

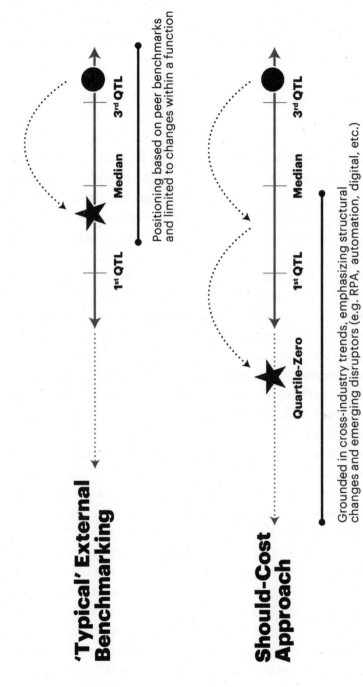

'Typical' External Benchmarking

1st QTL   Median   3rd QTL

Positioning based on peer benchmarks and limited to changes within a function

Should-Cost Approach

Quartile-Zero   1st QTL   Median   3rd QTL

Grounded in cross-industry trends, emphasizing structural changes and emerging disruptors (e.g. RPA, automation, digital, etc.)

Unsurprisingly, these new technologies change business processes so radically that they affect the entire P&L, advancing across all facets of ZBx and blurring the borders of their realms.

Shifting cost curves across ZBx realms

So far, only a small number of companies have begun to capture the fusion of human and machine skills. In doing so, they've laid the groundwork for reimagining their businesses, operating models and processes. They recognize that AI is not your typical capital investment: its value increases over time and it improves the value of people as well. When humans and machines are allowed to do what each does best, the result is a virtuous cycle of enhanced work that leads to increased productivity, a higher level of worker satisfaction and greater innovation.

Take General Electric as one example.[4] The company developed 'digital twins' of its deployed products, like the turbine blades of a jet engine. The company bases these virtual models on the current conditions of real machinery, enabling it to improve operations – the realm of ZBSC – as well as predict breakdowns before they occur – thus fundamentally changing how it maintains commercial equipment.

Sight Machine uses machine-learning analytics to enable its customers to reduce downtime when adding new machines to a factory floor.[5] In one case, the technology was able to reduce a customer's downtime (inherent in breaking in new robotic systems) by 50 per cent. In addition, the net gain was a 25 per cent increase in performance when all assets were up and running. The technology not only helps improve factory efficiency – the realm of ZBSC – but also allows engineers and maintenance workers to spend more time tackling other, high-value tasks – the realm of ZBO.

Robots from Symbiotic use machine vision algorithms to assess and pick oddly shaped or damaged boxes.[6] They measure shelf space to confirm that a box will fit, and immediately remove products from pallets and put them on shelves, eliminating the need for conveyor belts and space for pallet storage. This saved space can be used for additional shelf space – think ZBSC – and, in best-case scenarios, a warehouse can either store twice as many goods as before or operate in an area about 50 per cent smaller, fitting more easily into existing neighbourhoods. And perishable items can be stored closer to their point of sale – that's ZBC.

Coca-Cola piloted a proof-of-concept project using AI to manage its cooler cabinets in which its soft drinks were refrigerated at retail outlets worldwide. The project called for the deployment of a new AI capability, called Einstein, from customer relationship management (CRM) vendor Salesforce.[7] An Einstein-powered app allows on-site employees to take a photo of the cooler cabinet on their phone and Einstein's image-recognition services will analyse it and perform inventory control. Einstein can predict and recommend a restocking order, using CRM data and other information including weather forecasts, promotional offers, inventory levels and historical data to factor in seasonal fluctuations and various other parameters.[8] The automation of the count and restocking order saves employees paperwork and time – ZBO – and the added intelligence of the system has the potential to improve sales and increase customer satisfaction – ZBC.[9]

Companies that use AI to augment their human talent while reimagining their business processes achieve step gains in performance, propelling themselves to the forefront of their industries. Firms that continue deploying AI only as a way to automate may see some performance benefits, but those improvements will eventually stall. We predict that, within the next decade, a vast competitive advantage will emerge based not on *whether* an organization has implemented AI, but on *how* it has implemented it.

While changing established ways of working is daunting, embedding a ZBx culture centred on what things should be, rather than what they have been, pays off beyond the business case.[10] So how can you get on the path to quartile-zero thinking?

There are a couple of important things to consider. One is to map out how you can engage ecosystem partners to accelerate building the capabilities you'll need to make quartile zero work (see sidebar). The current pace of technology means that partnering with start-ups can give you an advantage in understanding new solutions in the market and give your company a quick win. And it's vital to understand the structure, processes and interactions between humans and machines necessary to optimize the technologies to meet the organization's needs.

SIDEBAR: The ecosystem effect on cost curves

An ecosystem is defined by the depth and breadth of potential collaboration among a set of players: each can deliver a piece of the solution or contribute a necessary capability. The power of the ecosystem is that no single player need own or operate all components of the solution, and that the value the ecosystem generates is larger than the combined value each of the players could contribute individually. Companies are forming ecosystems to make major innovation plays – delivering new products and services that grow the customer base and drive expansion into new markets. For instance, Adidas and Siemens are working together to build an intelligent manufacturing plant, or 'speed-factory', that can create customized shoes faster – and at a lower cost – than traditional methods, radically shifting cost curves and boosting growth.[11]

Shifting cost curves with ZBSC

So, exactly how does it work to shift cost curves by using a quartile-zero approach? Let's take the supply chain as one example. Only one-third of operations executives strongly agree that they see the results of their cost-reduction initiatives reflected in their P&L statements. Even fewer (18 per cent) are confident that leadership has the right initiatives in progress to achieve cost-reduction targets.[12] That's because companies are trapped in a supply-chain cost-reduction death spiral we touched on in the last chapter. They chase incremental savings when they could be radically shifting cost curves, boosting performance across the supply chain and creating new value to fuel sustained growth.

The adaptive nature of ZBSC reflects the fact that it does not rely on past performance or even first-quartile benchmarks from the past. It continually strives to develop a new quartile zero to set and stretch performance targets. Compare this with existing continuous improvement programmes. By the time a company makes the necessary improvements to meet historical benchmarks, those benchmarks have advanced. With ZBSC, companies apply digital technologies and sustainability practices that optimize price and performance across global operations and enable richer data insight and value.

Through ZBSC, companies embrace sustainability to reset supply-chain categories such as utilities, raw materials and packaging. Consider how Nike designed a line of clothing using materials from old items and transformed them into new, high-performance gear. The company used an average of 82 per cent recycled polyester fabric and up to an average of thirteen recycled plastic bottles in their uniforms, both of which dramatically affected the costs of raw materials across these product lines – reducing spend and driving profitability.[13]

By thinking outside the box and embracing technology, analytics and sustainability to set zero-quartile goals, companies can future-proof the operations. Look at maintenance costs. Predictive maintenance includes collecting information on such aspects as usage, wear and other asset-condition readings from disparate sources. Insight from sensor data enables early notification of possible failures, based on statistical models applied to historical data of the specific assets being monitored, preventing unplanned downtime and production losses.

Quartile zero leverages machine learning to update and improve its accuracy in identifying specific failure patterns. And it gives recommendations based on data and information on the operational KPIs, early warning alerts, root-causes analysis, etc.

We can also look at quartile-zero thinking applied to the last-mile delivery, with smart lockers located at convenient locations like metro stations and commercial complexes for easy delivery and pickup. The smart lockers are equipped with a card payment terminal and are placed in secure areas monitored remotely using CCTV cameras. Customers receive passwords to unlock them. The benefits are clear and include reduced delivery costs, investment and employee effort.

Shifting cost curves with ZBO

It's not only the COGS curve that can be shifted by applying should-cost (quartile-zero) models.[14] In a zero-based organization (ZBO) approach, by emphasizing work that is specifically customer facing, revenue generating or differentiated, companies are able to automate, consolidate or eliminate activities that are non-value-adding.

Let's start with finance, where the order-to-cash (OTC) process directly touches the customer. Applied intelligence such as self-service customer portals can improve the collection experience and cognitive agents can reduce dispute-resolution cycle time. Digital helps OTC by making it:

- **Automated** Robotics can even solve complex cases based on historical patterns across multiple data sources. In OTC a rate of 'untouched perfect orders' (i.e. without any manual intervention) of over 90 per cent should be a reasonable target in the near future.
- **Predictive** A digital control tower can provide information about imminent out-of-stock conditions that can lead to lost sales. Leading companies use predictive analytics combined with online store data and internal marketing insights to generate sales orders automatically. Collection functions can gain insights about future customer payments. These predictive capabilities help OTC functions proactively to identify issues and mitigate their impact.
- **Connected** A connected approach enables a new revenue growth management capability to holistically optimize company commercial investments (i.e. promotions, price, trade terms and product portfolio). This further connects commercial and marketing processes and can help increase profits.
- **Global** Global companies require global OTC that supports their expansion plans both through entering new countries and through acquisitions. Standardization is key. Yet one size does not fit all. In one multinational company with products in multiple categories, three OTC models were defined to address the diverse requirements of a multitude of countries.

Robotic process automation (RPA) is gaining strength. When implemented at scale, RPA payback can take as little as three to six months.[15] How? By letting organizations automate current tasks across applications and systems. Evolving from desktop automation over the past decade, RPA is now deployed in all industries: companies are using digital assistants to manage resources and staff for peak volumes. The ability to deliver accurate responses reduces the costs associated with human errors.

In human resources, employee experience is everything. In a world of hyper-connected employees, digital is a key enabler to that experience. Research shows that companies already use internal collaboration tools, predictive employee services and self-service apps that create consumer-like experiences.[16] And when companies get employee experience right, they outperform their peers on several important dimensions including customer loyalty (+17 per cent) and revenue (+11 per cent).[17]

How about procurement? By applying a zero-based spend approach, teams can leverage digital as-a-service models to fast-track strategic performance. As digital business services mature, subscribing to bot-enabled procurement can alleviate buyers' transactional loads, freeing them for more strategic pursuits – and funds for reinvestment in a more innovative procurement function. Strategic procurement professionals will instead work with the business to drive value creation in a new model by scouting the market for suppliers that enable digital business strategies.[18] Thanks to cloud and cognitive computing, RPA, the industrial internet of things (IIoT) and predictive analytics, the future cost of running procurement is projected to decrease by a whopping 40 to 60 per cent.[19]

Within IT, ZBx realigns people away from legacy work and towards more innovative and growth-driven initiatives that directly advance business objectives. Across the organization, it also enables employees to shift focus to the strategic, future-focused technology capabilities that are becoming increasingly central to all areas of an organization. By starting fresh, organizations can free themselves from the rigid, rear-facing structures that supported them in the past, and architect the flexible, 'boundaryless' ecosystems that will propel them into the future.

Take user support and front-line services: as automation technologies and AI solutions take on an increasingly large portion of this work, companies can significantly reduce their costs while providing consistently excellent customer service. They can also shift employees away from the transactional aspect of their roles into work that allows them to establish a connection with business users and drive a more personalized experience.[20]

Organizations are also applying the zero-based mindset to IT infrastructure and shifting more work to cloud solutions such as Amazon Web Services. By moving away from physical data centres, companies can migrate from a fixed-cost model to one that is pay-as-you-go and scalable. In organizations that understand how this shift affects the operating model, we also see critical thinking about the skillsets needed to support this new way of working, and about how these future-forward talent profiles differ from those required today.

Shifting cost curves with ZBS and ZBC

In facilities management, new technologies such as virtual reality headsets, digitally connected services and smart meeting and sharing applications reduce the number of physical meetings and associated costs. What's more, space can be optimized using geographic information system (GIS) technology that generates insights into space utilization. GIS, in turn, guides facility managers in making better use of office space, maximizing employees' productivity and providing a workplace perfectly suited to employee needs.

Connected lighting systems with sensors that measure light, temperature, energy consumption and occupancy can adapt to people and natural light, generating energy-cost savings. Intelligent security systems can replace manned security with, for example, smart cameras and robots acting as security guards. Smart tracking technology like smart waste bins that monitor fill levels in real time, and people counters that detect how many users have been in toilets in one hour, determine the most efficient use of cleaning resources.

Virtual assistants (VAs) with embedded natural language processing software – Siri, Alexa and WhatsApp or Facebook Chat, for example – use AI decision-tree technology to help resolve issues, handle transactions and respond to inquiries. Interaction occurs through voice calls or online chat bots. VAs use customer demographics, historical touchpoints and real-time channel interaction data to predict the intent of the interaction and drive personalization. The benefits: fewer agents and more customer satisfaction, among many others.

Going beyond online interactions, robots with vocal, facial, gender and emotional recognition can communicate with customers, recommend the best products according to their preferences and offer special promotions or discounts. They help automate and increase the speed and quality of the sales process and transform and improve customer experience with personalized services, brand promotion and augmented and virtual reality.

The art of the possible

In the end, quartile zero isn't about moving along a cost curve to incrementally improve a position – i.e. making a process a little faster and more efficient or reducing headcount by a percentage point or two. It involves thinking about the art of what's possible: how today's advanced digital technologies can enable what has not been possible before, so that companies can completely redefine their cost curve. Its growing success means the days of traditional benchmark-driven cost-reduction approaches are numbered.[21]

4. 'The way we *should* do things around here'

'Culture'. It's a word with a multitude of definitions. For many companies, culture is simply what's usual. Or, 'The way we do things around here.' Success with ZBx involves zero-basing the culture, creating a fresh value system across the company where all employees feel like a business owner and make decisions accordingly. With ZBx, culture is about enabling, 'The way we *should* do things around here.'

It requires engendering accountability throughout all levels of the organization, a concept that's at the very core of ZBx. Without accountability, internal mechanisms are bypassed. Good intentions slip. Before you know it, the old way of doing business creeps back and subsumes hard-won gains. But with ZBx, cost and spend management become a continuous process that fosters teamwork around return on investment (ROI) and budgetary goals. People are held accountable for categories of spend, and they are encouraged to treat the company's money like their own so that they question the value of each dollar.[1]

Accountability begins and ends with leaders throughout the organization who reinforce a sense of ownership and entrepreneurship company-wide. If that sounds soft and fluffy, let's make it more concrete. There are three levers leaders can pull to evolve the corporate culture, creating a vehicle that perpetuates ZBx, making organizations impervious to the vagaries of marketplace dynamics.[2]

First lever: Set the tone from the top, or 'show and tell'

'Tone' is the operative word here. Effective ZBx leadership is not about firing off top-down mandates but more about the way leaders speak and act. With a tone that's direct. Authentic. Transparent. Because when it comes to change, people don't believe in a new direction because they suspend disbelief: the behaviour, action and results that they see lead them to conclude that the new capability will work.

Let's face it, leaders and employees view change differently. Leaders typically see change as an opportunity for both the business and themselves, while employees typically see it as disruptive, intrusive and likely to involve loss. By communicating too late or inconsistently, leaders end up alienating the people who are most affected by the changes.

To avoid this, a good transformation story that bridges the gap between top management and the rest of the organization is required. Typically using metaphors and analogies to explain what is at stake, the transformation story addresses three aspects of ZBx: the case for change, the challenges and opportunities ahead, and the impact of change on individuals. The story should be written by the leadership in prose, not bullet points.

Good stories also confront the emotional angle – the need to bid farewell to cherished habits and routines and to embrace a different, and perhaps initially uncomfortable, future. Leaders should tailor the story to their audience, invoking the organization's heritage to inspire loyalty and affection and injecting their own personalities into what they say or write. Again, tone is critical, so sharing feelings and personal-development goals in an open, honest, even humble way enhances a leader's credibility and authenticity.

Consider difficult issues like headcount reductions. They often engender fear. It's important to take care when communicating to employees why layoffs are necessary. And to detail how every vested interest that is cut can be linked to an opportunity for doing something better in the future. People are more likely to come aboard when they understand that they will end up working in a less bureaucratic workplace and in a company poised for growth.

The onus is on leaders to explain how ZBx will work, who will drive it, its alignment with the organization's strategy, the intended outcomes, and how it affects the staff. They must build confidence in the success of ZBx to encourage company-wide buy-in that will lead to accountability. This is especially important if the organization suffers from change fatigue from past efforts, aggravated by a lack of confidence in its ability to implement strategic initiatives successfully.

Second lever: Activate leaders – changing 'The way we do things around here'

One of the most critical factors for successful organizational change is how well senior executives visibly live and breathe new ways of working. Leaders must actively encourage the entire organization to do the same through engaging and compelling communications and leading by example: acting as role models, setting a credible and meaningful example of what is expected of others in embracing successful change. When people we trust and admire clearly model and encourage new behaviours, those behaviours spread much more quickly. And, importantly, they stick.

Take the case of a major global food manufacturer. They encouraged employees to act as if they were owners of the company to instil personal responsibility, particularly in the area of smart spending. The company reinvested savings generated from employee owners into ideas involving new product development, growth and bolstering digital capabilities.

While leaders can model examples of desired behaviours in their day-to-day interactions and enlist help from influential employees at all levels to champion the change, new behaviours must be authentic. Change efforts seen as lip service from senior management are doomed.

'It's not the culture change aspect that might make you shy away from ZBx. It's the ambition needed.'

– CEO OF AN ELECTRONICS COMPANY

Third lever: Hardwiring behaviour in corporate DNA

ZBx dramatically changes the way people work. For example, a new spend governance model called category ownership (see Chapter 8) is implemented in the organization, creating a healthy tension between different groups of people who are simultaneously accountable for every dollar spent: an entity owner and a cost category owner. Before ZBx, most companies had only one budget owner.

Also, a zero-based, bottom-up approach to budgeting helps hardwire the new mindset. People go from complaining about reductions over last year's budget to defending exactly what resources they need to get things done. From a use-it-or-lose-it approach to a return-on-investments mindset. These aspects of ZBx will be discussed in further detail in Part II.

On the other hand, it might be tempting to run ZBx as a 'programme' that includes plenty of rules, processes, boxes to check, forms to fill out and spreadsheets to monitor. And while the process aspect of smart spending is very real, leading with it spells disaster. Downplaying rules, and emphasizing mindset and behaviours, bodes much better for the overall success of ZBx.[3] And mutates the company's DNA.

That's why hardwiring also calls for paying attention to the repeated attitudes and behaviour of leaders and employees. Even small changes in behaviour can create a ripple effect through an organization as others see their value and follow suit. Emphasize the positive, make opportunities relatable and appeal to social proof, i.e. 'Here's what others just like you are already doing, to reinforce the adoption of new norms.' People unconsciously imitate what others do. This is particularly true among colleagues.

Mutual respect is a powerful source of influence. People listen when information is communicated by teammates with whom they work closely and often. Highlighting everyday heroes who shave costs or reinvent more efficient processes works. Igniting a network of champions can help build organizational buy-in around new roles, tools and ways of working.

Recognizing and rewarding the right behaviour is a basic behavioural-science principle. Organizations can reinforce desired changes by setting individual and organizational performance goals. And motivating people through both financial and non-financial incentives – the 'carrot' rather than the 'stick' – so they align with the changes wrought through ZBx: from giving people a portion of the savings they identify, to creating forums where they can share ideas and successes, to highlighting champions of the cause.

Companies should work with HR leadership to map the employee lifecycle and so understand the touchpoints where new standards and behaviours should be embedded. They can do this by making new policies a core part of employee onboarding or by writing new behaviours into formal job descriptions. Newer employee-engagement techniques are available to integrate desired actions into everyday performance. One major global food manufacturer recently encouraged employees to act as an owner of the company would – weighing each decision against the merits for all involved.[4]

Directed programmes over a short time period – as little as one month – can use discrete performance challenges or 'micro actions' to help employees perform in new ways while also bonding with their colleagues toward a common goal. A set of thirty daily micro-challenges enabled by enterprise social media enforces on-the-job learning and can help employees do their jobs in new ways. Participants receive, complete and reflect upon daily challenges in a chat-like interface, and view peer insights and progress. Gaming elements engender competition, maintain engagement and embed learning.

Organizations may struggle with sustaining ZBx if they fail to hardwire behaviour into the corporate DNA. Here are four key questions to steer them back in the right direction:

- How will they develop and sustain new ways of working?
- How will new behaviours be embedded into reward and incentive structures?
- How will colleagues and teams be recognized and celebrated for success?
- Where should ZBx culture be embedded in the employee journey?

The linchpin of change

It's ironic. The C-suite gets the most praise for an organization's success while team leadership is lauded as the foundation for getting work done. Yet research shows the most important role for implementing change lies with the business unit leaders, or divisional heads.[5]

Research studying nearly one million employees involved in change initiatives at 150 global corporations identified ten major drivers of successful change. These included vision and direction, communication, business and team leadership, skills and staffing, systems and processes, accountability and a broad range of emotions. Of those drivers, business leadership had, by far, the most significant impact on business performance (improvements in effectiveness, customer service, cost management etc.) as well as a substantial effect on realizing benefits. In addition, all of the other major drivers of change are themselves driven either primarily or indirectly by business leadership. In essence, nothing budges without first being nurtured, nudged, pushed, or prodded by the middle layers. Collectively, they are the linchpin connecting the top and bottom of the organization.

From the top down, they translate the corporate vision into terms that staffers can relate to and, more importantly, embrace. And from the bottom up, they ensure that the teams below them receive the communication they need, and have the accountability, positive emotions and resources necessary to do their jobs well.

Keeping ZBx in the loop

Building a culture that keeps people doing the right thing takes everything outlined in this chapter and more. That 'more' is a closed-loop process that drives full visibility on all operating spend – across business units, categories and geographies to a detailed level – and explores how the money can be spent more wisely to add enterprise value and strengthen a company's competitiveness. In the next part of this book we'll sample the 'secret sauce' of ZBx: the closed-loop approach.

PART II

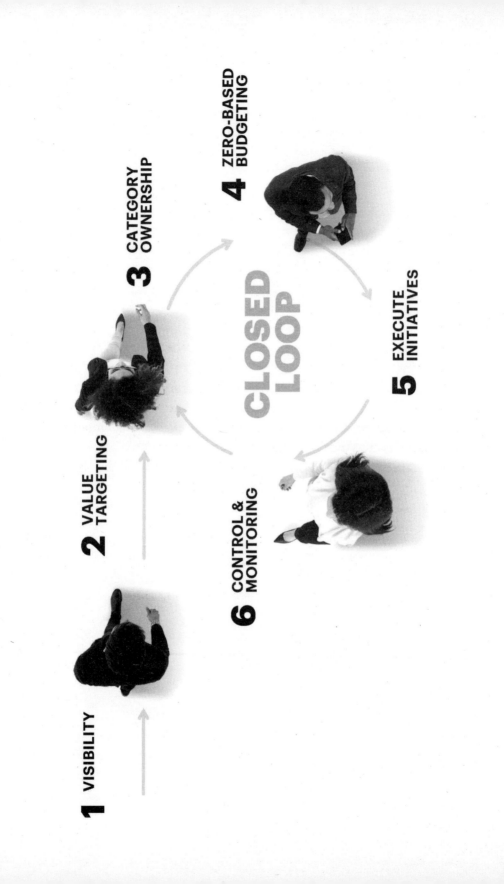

1 VISIBILITY

2 VALUE TARGETING

3 CATEGORY OWNERSHIP

4 ZERO-BASED BUDGETING

5 EXECUTE INITIATIVES

6 CONTROL & MONITORING

CLOSED LOOP

5. A Taste of the Secret Sauce

Now that we've covered the high-level background and strategy behind the zero-based mindset, we'll move into the capabilities needed to master it, moving ZBx from a one-off to a strategic and durable management technique. Key to the latter is establishing what we call the ZBx closed loop. This is the secret sauce of making the zero-based mindset successful and sustainable.

Think of the ZBx closed loop as a virtuous cycle of self-reinforcing insight and action that constantly challenges how resources are allocated against strategic intent. There are six ingredients that, combined, drive full P&L visibility at a consistent level of detail across each part of an organization; that stake out clear ownership for each dollar and are the catalysts for culture change that embeds accountability into the consciousness of an organization.

Here are the six parts of the loop we'll explore in the next chapters:

- **Driving visibility** Simply put, this is about establishing a baseline. It's first in the loop because it serves as the foundation for everything within ZBx. Because how can you transform an organization if you don't first see it – warts and all? This step provides forensic insight into 'bad' and 'good' cost. It enables transformation by shifting mindsets from perception and organizational myths to cold hard facts about the state of operations. Establishing 'one version of the truth' upon which all efforts are driven.
- **Value targeting** In a nutshell, value targeting is about ambition and continually opening gaps in performance and finding ways to close them. This capability explores factors like the impact of financial performance, and

which strategies require investment to what degree. Through it, companies develop a culture of continuous innovation around the areas of cost efficiency and revenue growth.

- **Category ownership** ZBx creates an unprecedented level of accountability to outcomes decided in the value targeting phase. How? Through a model marked by a duality of perception on cost that fosters a 'healthy tension' between category and entity owners. This tension expands and accelerates the potential to realize its ambition.

- **Lock targets into the budget** A zero-based budget links resources to strategic priorities, operationalizing the ambition across the organization. In effect, the budgeting process is a glue that enables planning, motivation, evaluation and coordination that gets everyone pulling on the same oar. And because budgeting solidifies ownership, it reinforces accountability. Ultimately, this phase connects top-down ambition with bottom-up operational plans enabling organizations to quickly and efficiently scale to meet challenges and, in the process, gain a competitive advantage.

- **Execute initiatives** A company's strategy breaks down when it's executed poorly. That's why this capability is arguably the most difficult within the closed loop. Because, through ZBx, companies spawn thousands of initiatives, each requiring resources, management and measurement.

- **Control and monitoring** ZBx isn't a 'one and done' approach. It's a management technique that's durable over time. Control and monitoring is a capability that makes an organization perpetually vigilant about sustaining visibility and results, and willing to take corrective steps to get things back on track should they derail.

Making the sauce hotter

The closed-loop approach is a secret sauce that gets hotter when you add digital tools. How? Cloud-based, global collaboration tools can transform how companies lock cost targets into budgets and control spend. They centralize the collection and analysis of spend for a single version of the truth. With the right business intelligence and data analysis tools, users don't have to be data scientists to wield them to drive savings insights. Over time, this business intelligence becomes the basis for feeding AI and machine-learning algorithms that predict zero-based budgets with an increasing level of accuracy.

Take data visibility as another example. It's a major headache for nearly every company on the planet. No wonder, considering that nearly a quarter of them still use spreadsheets for their cost-related reporting.[1] By replacing spreadsheets with automation and AI technologies, companies can dramatically improve data visibility as well as data quality, KPIs and processes.

Now onto a deeper dive into visibility in the next chapter.

CLOSED LOOP

1 VISIBILITY

2 VALUE TARGETING

3 CATEGORY OWNERSHIP

4 ZERO-BASED BUDGETING

5 EXECUTE INITIATIVES

6 CONTROL & MONITORING

6. Driving Visibility – Moving from Denial to Acceptance

The psychiatrist Elisabeth Kübler-Ross codified the five stages of grief as 'denial, anger, bargaining, depression and acceptance'.[1] Driving visibility in an organization can prompt a similar grieving process: when executives first see the reality behind how much is being spent and where, the first reaction is denial, with anger coming in a close second.

But moving from denial to acceptance is when culture change begins. Because without a clear picture of reality, change is impossible. Visibility enables transformation by shifting organizational mindsets from perception to cold hard reality, establishing 'one version of the truth' upon which all efforts are driven.

Each type of ZBx approach – zero-based spend (ZBS), zero-based organization (ZBO), zero-based supply chain (ZBSC) and zero-based commercial (ZBC) – focuses on gaining visibility into different P&L categories. And each category carries its own unique challenges.[2] Let's start with ZBS, which covers all non-people-related G&A expenses. Consider this: a company's chart of accounts may lack sufficient granularity. And account definitions may be unclear or missing, with costs misclassified or hidden in other areas of the P&L. What's more, cost-related data is often stored in different formats or classifications in different locations.

In most companies, the number of transactions analysed will number in the millions. And usually 20–35 per cent of costs are re-allocated. The task of categorizing these transactions is daunting, to say the least. AI tools can take this scattered data and leverage algorithms that rapidly classify the data, providing a harmonized, single source of truth. The result: the true SG&A baseline is often 20–40 per cent higher than executives believe.[3]

ZBO covers all people-related overhead expenses. Companies

usually address organizational change from a functional or cost-centre perspective, which limits their ability to transform an entire process and the outcome it can generate. ZBO focuses on end-to-end employee processes and the outcomes they are delivering for the organization. In fact, a company may have finance or HR people in its business units who generally won't be included in an analysis of finance or HR. If not addressed, this situation limits the potential result.

The ZBO methodology focuses on understanding the entire process, irrespective of functional boundaries. It maps employees to the right process, independent of the function or cost centre they're assigned to. This creates a better understanding of the organization's costs, which leads to better insights and decision making during the value targeting and organizational design phases.

ZBSC covers COGS, variable manufacturing and logistics costs, as well as fixed operating costs that are embedded into the manufacturing or logistics network. The sheer volume and complexity of transactions involved with the design, production, movement and servicing of products is staggering. This complexity results in data sets that don't follow a common taxonomy for products, parts, assets and equipment, which slows the ability to get and process information at a detailed level.

Supply-chain leaders depend on facility and business leads to process the data to give them a summary-level view of performance. The problem is, this view holds historical performance based on what happened, not what 'should be'.

ZBC covers sales, marketing, trade spend and pricing opportunities. The ZBC closed-loop approach provides deep visibility into all commercial components to identify, eliminate and prevent unproductive activities on an ongoing basis. It helps companies address the main problem with optimizing commercial costs: namely, that it often compromises customer experience. This triggers switching and churn, which in turn ultimately results in a net-negative impact on the P&L. Great customer experience is critical to customer value: satisfied customers have been proven to drive profitability by buying more, trying more, repurchasing more, staying longer with the provider, forgiving more and advocating more.

With that in mind, ZBC enables companies to develop the P&L of each customer to assess the actual value of the overall customer base, including the value of each experience. These insights highlight the relative value contributions of each customer and drive precise customer experience interventions. The net result: ZBC helps a company monetize loyalty, minimize service costs, churn and bad debt, optimize pricing and improve customer experience.

Begin with the baseline

Driving visibility is all about having a level of transparency that credibly fosters the consensus needed to move forward in establishing targets. And to challenge everyone involved to think differently about what is needed and how it is achieved. The process of creating one drives an extra benefit: it raises the consciousness of stakeholders when it comes to current costs. Entity owners rarely have detailed knowledge of where their money is actually going and are usually in denial when they find out. The baseline helps them identify and understand the steps they need to take and the behaviours they need to change to secure an efficient cost base in the future.

The first step towards establishing a solid baseline is to analyse the annotated chart of accounts. The chart of accounts should serve as the correct representation of a company's financial situation. A balanced middle ground between visibility (the number of accounts) and relevance (the amount in each account) should be enforced. Also, the names, annotations and explanations of each account should be clear enough for any non-expert to understand what spending should be posted where.

Because most users of the chart of accounts are not accountants, and are usually inexperienced at interpreting a general ledger, they naturally tend to make mistakes when confronted with ambiguous account names. As a result, users may erroneously post their spending in a generic account such as 'Other' or 'Miscellaneous'.

In most cases, between 80 and 90 per cent of the spending accounted as 'Miscellaneous' should have been posted to a more specific account. Eliminating or minimizing postings to catch-all accounts is of paramount importance to ZBx for two reasons:

- Benchmarking entities that correctly account their own spending against those entities that do not will produce biased results, penalizing those with the correct accounting.
- Budget targets set according to the spending level of the faulty entities may be artificially low and unattainable for everyone else. As a result, they can promote internecine battles between entity owners during different phases.

The hierarchy of entities should be analysed and aligned with the most up-to-date organization chart. If entities don't match up with the organization chart, the hierarchy needs to be updated. Because ZBx is characterized by a shifting of resources to fund innovation and profitability, accountability is crucial. It's critical that all cost in the ZBx scope can be correctly traced back to the parties responsible for spending it. There are two different ways of handling cost, according to whether it's direct or indirect:[4]

- As the name suggests, direct costs can be traced back to the entity that generated the cost. The most common examples of direct costs include labour and materials.
- Typically, anything that cannot be classified as a direct cost gets classified as an indirect cost. Indirect costs are generally placed into one of two categories: overhead or SG&A.

That's straightforward enough. But the process of tracing indirect costs to specific entities is anything but direct. Most organizations use some method of allocation. One example is 'seat charges' that capture consumption of IT, energy, etc. Allocations such as these clearly contain a wide margin of wiggle room, creating the potential to grossly misstate the true costs of specific entities.

To foster accountability, ZBx treats direct and indirect costs differently from the standard practice, especially overhead costs. How? By using the controllability principle, which means that it's only appropriate to charge those costs that are significantly influenced by the manager of a given entity. The controllability principle can be implemented either by eliminating the uncontrollable items from the areas for which managers are held accountable or by calculating their effects so that the reports distinguish between controllable and uncontrollable items.[5]

When it comes to evaluating individual managers under ZBx, it's best to remove the effects of costs or circumstances that entity owners have little or no control over. Examples include corporate overhead, research and development expenses, or gains and losses due to fluctuations in foreign exchange rates.

Uncontrollable expenses should be accounted for in the entities that are ultimately responsible for them – and who can act to reduce expenses. Examples are entities from the corporate centre for the corporate overhead, R&D entities for the corporate research and development expenses, and the treasury entity for fluctuations in foreign exchange rates.

The ZBx baseline (and subsequent cost monitoring and management) should be calculated before allocations of uncontrollable costs. This shouldn't prevent the organization from making cost allocations afterward for things like product or service costing or cost-to-serve. Instead it allows the organization to take a snapshot of the financial situation before the allocations are made and use this picture frozen in time for ZBx purposes.

'Zero-based budgeting is a systematic approach, not a one-time event. It's all about ownership and doing more with less. It drives accountability and encourages our employees to treat company dollars as if they are their own.'

– CEO OF A GLOBAL CPG COMPANY[6]

Entities

Entities are the lowest-level units for which budgets are prepared and monitored, but still of material size to the organization. They're an aggregate of cost centres and profit or investment centres (the 'responsibility centres') under the control of a single manager.

Entities replicate the organizational chart down to department-manager level. And they consolidate budgets under coordinators, supervisors and so forth. That means learning and development managers would be in charge of an entity that aggregates the budget for which they are responsible as well as those of their regional supervisors. Peers managed by the human resources director would similarly consolidate their supervisors' budgets as well as their own. On the other hand, the HR director's entity would have only their own budget and not consolidate those of the managers below. The same principle applies to the upper levels of the organization.

Some organizations may choose to implement the mindset only in select businesses, divisions or functions to target specific areas of need and limit resources. Naturally, only those entities in the division where ZBx will be piloted or implemented should be in scope.

Finally, it's important to segregate the entities used for projects and non-business-as-usual activities and expenditures from the

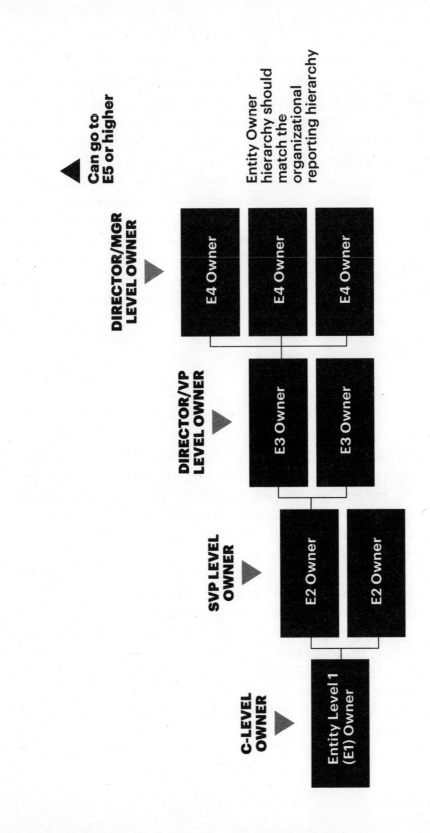

C-LEVEL OWNER

Entity Level 1 (E1) Owner

SVP LEVEL OWNER

E2 Owner

E2 Owner

DIRECTOR/VP LEVEL OWNER

E3 Owner

E3 Owner

DIRECTOR/MGR LEVEL OWNER

E4 Owner

E4 Owner

E4 Owner

Can go to E5 or higher

Entity Owner hierarchy should match the organizational reporting hierarchy business-as-usual entities. This segregation is essential for building an appropriate baseline upon which decisions will be made and against which savings will be measured. Contamination of business-as-usual accounts by project and once-only expenditures is a major source of misunderstandings (and misinformed targets and budgeting).

This segregation also enables better visibility of project expenditures such as personnel, contractors, consultants and travel, and an adequate and comparable assessment of the ROI of each project as well as proper budget versus actual comparison of projects and business-as-usual expenditures.

The zero-based mindset fosters continuous improvement cycles. Because of that, it can only be applied to entities with active leaders willing to step up to the challenge. With that noted, entities for discontinued facilities or for businesses on the verge of a divestiture should not be the focus of ZBx.

Mapping general ledger accounts

Cost categories are the aggregate of accounts of a similar nature and theme within a general ledger, of material size to the organization, and that usually (but not always) are common to several entities. They drive forensically detailed and standardized visibility into an organization's spending and are used to account for and control the use of resources.

There is no one-size-fits-all number of cost categories as the trade-off between visibility, accountability and complexity, and materiality is different in each organization. With that noted, they usually range between twenty and thirty. Some of the most common cost categories include everything from salaries and overtime to maintenance and logistics.

Some companies classify cost categories differently depending on their ZBx scope, but there are three types: simple, complex and variable.

Simple categories are usually of a fixed nature with decentralized purchasing decisions. Savings are gained by behavioural change and enforcement of new standards and guidelines with minimal risks to the business. Global consistency of rules throughout divisions is expected. Good examples are benefits and other personnel expenditures, travel and legal expenses and institutional cost categories.

Complex categories may be fixed or semi-variable to volume (either sales or production) and usually include spending of a more technical nature with centralized purchasing decisions. Savings are often related to efficiency improvements since reckless budget cuts in these areas can pose an existential risk to the business. Good examples are salaries and overtime, sales and marketing, maintenance and distribution and logistics.

Variable categories are directly linked to volume levels (either sales or production) and savings are related to efficiency improvements. Good examples are raw materials and non-overhead utilities categories.

Aligning people

Management across the business gets involved as expenditures and programmes are evaluated at a forensic level. Finance and procurement work together as management examines who spends how much on what. They answer questions like 'Is the investment maximizing the return?'

This is true for both personnel and other costs. But the correct allocation of personnel is much harder to confirm because the speed of change in reporting lines is often faster than that of updates to human resources and payroll systems. As a result, systems are usually outdated and don't reflect the current reality. And human resources and payroll systems aren't fully integrated into budgeting and accounting systems, creating a mismatch between organization charts, payroll and budget. Entities are charged personnel costs according to the payroll or cost allocations rather than actual reporting lines.

Until recently, most companies have been unable to gather global data in a consistent and accessible format. 'Just a few years ago, the mere task of calculating how many people worked for our company was a challenge,' noted James Stringer, HR Director of Unilever. 'Now that we have global data and systems, we can access that information at the click of a mouse. With such standardized and high-quality data, we have the firm foundation for analytic investigation.' If the largest companies have only just devoted the necessary resources to compiling HR data in an organized manner, smaller organizations are likely to have some way to go in this regard.[7]

Artificial intelligence can take mapping job titles to functional roles to the next level by learning and adapting to the idiosyncrasies of each area in an organization. What do we mean by that? Think about a financial analyst working in a plant. This person belongs in the finance function, but they will often be associated with the supply chain function when it comes to charting the organization.

A(I)ligning general ledger and accounts payable

Another challenge within visibility is at the line-item level. Twenty to 35 per cent of all costs need be reallocated because people do not use the chart of accounts properly or accounts are not granular enough.[8] So cross-referencing the general ledger with accounts-payable data is a must for driving clarity. Ensuring that spending has been correctly accounted for, and consistent data can be extracted, is of paramount importance to the ZBx process as a whole.

According to research,[9] nearly one-quarter of companies on their zero-based journey still use spreadsheets for reporting. Automated AI approaches industrialize the process with dramatically improved data visibility and data quality. By centralizing the collection and analysis of spend and supporting it with data visualization and analysis tools, companies can understand and apply the insights to make intelligent and efficient business decisions. This approach also helps facilitate the culture change that the adoption of a zero-based mindset requires by arming business owners with the data they need to make key decisions in real time on their path to sustainable growth.

Separating the recurring from the one-offs

Business is cyclical. Sometimes volatile. Plants shut down unexpectedly. Or get hit by force majeure. Consumer trends shift seemingly overnight. The end result: exceptional costs in the previous year, or new, unforeseen costs in the current one. All of these need to be identified and taken into consideration.

Costs can also be examined with respect to their frequency of occurrence (recurring versus non-recurring). Examples of non-recurring costs include project design, market assessment, capital investment, training, divestment and so on. Examples of recurring costs include material, direct labour, distribution, transportation, packaging and sales.[10]

It is critical to separate spending in recurring and non-recurring activities (especially projects) to arrive at a reliable historical business-as-usual database. This separation is necessary for better visibility of both project- and non-project-related spending, including personnel, contractors, consulting, travel etc. It also enables the correct assessment of each project's ROI, the comparison of expected spending, and ROI for projects and their subsequent prioritization or ranking. And, importantly, it facilitates the approval of new projects that haven't been budgeted for.

The business-as-usual database can be calculated as:

Actual previous year expenditures within the scope of ZBx
(−) One-time-only expenditures
(+/−) Non-permanent volume change
(+/−) Non-permanent scope change

(−) Non-permanent special projects
(=) Business-as-usual database

Understanding the variables

Once a good understanding of business-as-usual actual figures is arrived at, it's important to understand variations between budget and actual figures (current and past two-to-three years). A variations analysis needs to be conducted between the actual baseline business-as-usual figures and the current year's budget to understand the effects of inflation, seasonality, changes in scope and volume levels, special projects etc. Variation analysis also teases out ongoing cost-reduction initiatives that are already considered in the budget. The objective is to know everything from how good at budgeting a company is to which accounts are prone to variation and why. Whenever variations are too big or can't be explained by the finance team, then the entity owners should be questioned and challenged to drive a water-tight baseline.

The number of adjustments needed to create a realistic baseline from the previous year's costs is considerable – usually in the hundreds of thousands. While conceptually straightforward, it's labour intensive. And needs to be done methodically so that all adjustments are agreed upon and recorded with a clear bridge back to the starting P&L.

Artificial intelligence can certainly help. But it's still a daunting task involving multiple stakeholders. The effort is worth it: value comes not only from having an accurate position from which to move forward, but also from the education that the exercise delivers. It's the most effective way to reach the consensus and buy-in needed to proceed with a robust plan. As such, it's the foundation for the next capability in the closed loop: value targeting.

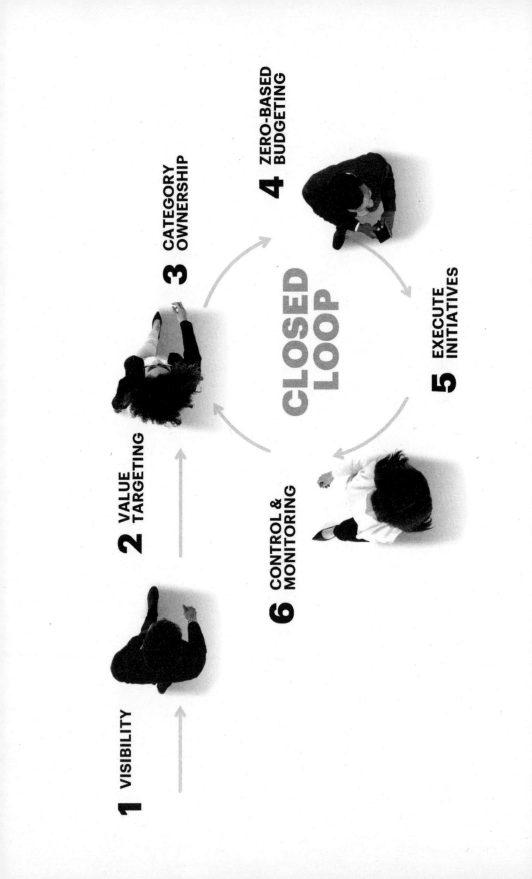

1 VISIBILITY

2 VALUE TARGETING

3 CATEGORY OWNERSHIP

4 ZERO-BASED BUDGETING

5 EXECUTE INITIATIVES

6 CONTROL & MONITORING

CLOSED LOOP

7. Value Targeting – Nailing the Ambition

Value targeting is all about nailing the ambition by quantifying the cost and revenue optimization potential of going zero-based. Along the way, value targeting creates a culture of continuous innovation around cost efficiency and revenue growth, profitability and trust. How? Consider a mundane example: a multinational's travel category. By minimizing the number of trips taken, the company saves, and those resources are funnelled into areas of growth. But in the bargain, the company also reduces its carbon footprint and contributes to the work–life balance of employees.

Value targeting works by using top-down benchmarking and bottom-up analyses to define improvement potential and specific initiatives for revenue, pricing, cost categories and cost drivers. It is a new capability that becomes business-as-usual as the company's culture adopts a zero-based mindset. The end goal: align a company's resources with its strategic priorities by replacing low-value-added activities (non-working money) with high-value-added activities (working money), boosting efficacy and efficiency, improving revenues and reducing costs.

Consider a software company that shifted from selling products to selling consumption to compete with more agile, cloud-based, competitors. Although the company's business model changed, its contact centre was still focused on customer tech support and things like driving down cost per call, reducing handling times and other metrics.

To boost margins, the company used zero-based thinking to redefine its entire approach to customer support. By stripping away all the old metrics and starting afresh with the one that mattered – product adoption – the company rewarded agents who spent more time providing insight to their customers about the product.

The result? A significantly higher consumption of the company's software without any material increase in operating costs. And more opportunity for growth and innovation as the entire focus of the organization turned to what mattered most.

The specific steps within value targeting are ongoing, not one-off, and involve cross-functional processes with three phases:

- **Open the gap** Determine KPIs and benchmark them against best-in-class companies to identify gaps. Opening the gap requires identification of those entities holding the greatest potential for performance improvement. Then run value targeting workshops to identify additional areas for improvement.
- **Monetize the gap** Calculate potential savings based on the difference between current and benchmark performance levels.
- **Close the gap** Identify initiatives to close the gap in performance, and review and select initiatives to be rolled out.

The first step, opening the gap, involves selecting cost categories and their KPIs. It's important to note that the definition of each KPI should be aligned across the organization so data will be comparable and benchmarking results will be applicable throughout.

Data is then collected through systems retrieval and site visits. And KPIs are calculated by performing a deep-dive analysis into the company's operations. Benchmarking (top-down targets) is done both internally (site-to-site within the company) and externally (against peers).

The value of workshops

Another way to open the gap is by holding yearly value targeting workshops with representatives from across the organization to discuss savings levers (bottom-up analysis). The owners of specific areas of the business – the people who live with it daily – are intimately involved in defining what the future looks like. This bottom-up approach sends a clear message to employees: we value your insight and want you to be a key partner in shaping the future. While it can take longer than top-down approaches, change sticks since it's designed by the people who carry it forward.

Value-targeting workshops are structured by cost category to highlight results, share best practices, identify new opportunities and discuss trade-offs between the potential uses of resources (such as working-money investment in marketing), the ROI of such resources and their alignment with the organization's strategy. Category owners and key stakeholders evaluate initiatives and define action plans that are then assigned to initiative owners.

Preparation is key to the success of these workshops. Ahead of time, it's important to identify and capture new opportunities to be considered, ensure that there's a list of initiatives against each cost category, and prepare 'cheat sheets' that include CAPEX and OPEX requirements and implementation timing.

During the workshop, existing initiatives are explored and brainstorming sessions are held to identify new ones. Then action plans are drawn up that quantify results, specify timing and justify resources. Finally, the output of these workshops is presented to other groups to address interdependencies that might have been overlooked. This work all feeds into the next phase of value targeting: monetize the gap (see sidebar on page 67). The deliverable of the workshop is an ROI tracker by P&L item detailing, for example, ownership, the annualized running rate of results for the next two to three years and forecasted results for the next four quarters (high level phasing). Ultimately, this output becomes the input for the budget (more on that later).

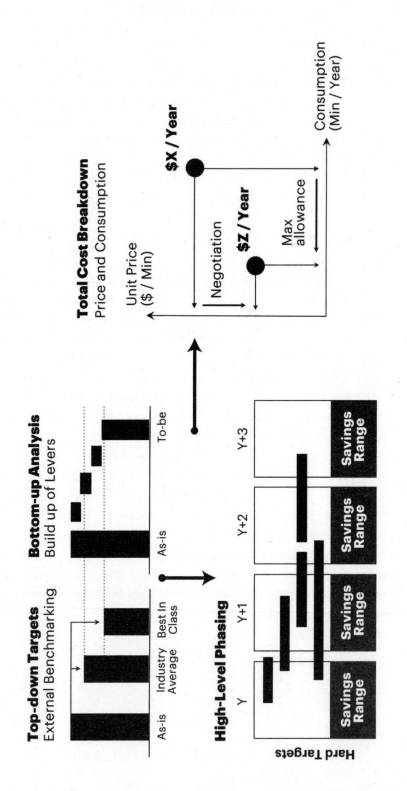

SIDEBAR: Inspiration for initiatives[1]

Value-generating initiatives aren't always easy to identify. Change concepts may be used as a broad provocation in brainstorming sessions to create a list of tangible and specific initiatives to close the gaps identified in value targeting and committed to in budgeting. In this sidebar we present a non-exhaustive list of change concepts to light the creative spark in your ZBx.

1. Eliminate waste

- Eliminate things that are not used
- Eliminate multiple entry
- Reduce or eliminate overkill
- Reduce controls on the system
- Recycle or reuse
- Use substitution
- Reduce classifications
- Remove intermediaries
- Match the amount to the need
- Use sampling
- Change targets or set points

2. Improve work flow

- Synchronize
- Schedule into multiple processes
- Minimize handoffs
- Move steps in the process close together
- Find and remove bottlenecks
- Use automation
- Smooth work flow
- Do tasks in parallel
- Consider people as the same system
- Use multiple processing units
- Adjust to peak demand

- Change the order of process steps

3. Optimize inventory

- Match inventory to predicted demand
- Use pull systems
- Reduce choices of features
- Reduce multiple brands of same item

4. Change the work environment

- Give people access to information
- Use proper measurements
- Take care of basics
- Reduce demotivating aspects of pay system
- Conduct training
- Implement cross-training
- Invest more resources in improvement

- Focus on core processes and purpose
- Share risks
- Emphasize natural and logical consequences
- Develop alliances/ cooperative relationships

5. Producer/customer interface

- Listen to customers
- Coach customers to use product/service
- Focus on the outcome to a customer
- Use a coordinator
- Reach agreement on expectations
- Outsource for 'free'
- Optimize level of inspection
- Work with suppliers

6. Focus on time

- Reduce setup or start-up time
- Set up timing to use discounts
- Optimize maintenance
- Extend specialists' time
- Reduce wait time

7. Focus on variation

- Standardize
- Stop tampering
- Develop operational definitions
- Improve predictions
- Develop contingency plans
- Sort products into grades
- Desensitize
- Exploit variation

8. Eliminate mistakes

- Use reminders
- Use differentiation
- Use constraints
- Use affordances

9. Focus on the product or service

- Mass customize
- Offer product/service any time
- Offer product/service any place
- Emphasize intangibles
- Influence or take advantage of fashion trends
- Reduce the number of component parts
- Differentiate product using quality dimensions

Why are brainstorming sessions so important for creating initiatives? Because it's human nature for people to prefer to come up with solutions themselves rather than be told what to do. It increases the probability of making the behavioural change and new way of working durable. It also enables a company to achieve outcomes faster: if people are involved in creating the initiative, they own it, making them more committed and accountable. Which in turn makes it easier and quicker for them to decide to implement the changes.

The monetize-the-gap step uses input from the open-the-gap step and the visibility exercise to provide an overview of results across the company. The potential savings are the difference between the current and benchmark levels multiplied by the unit price and quantity of a specific cost item.

How does that look? Take the savings in the cost of water in a production plant, for example. They would equal the difference in water-usage ratios (water consumption divided by production volume) between current and benchmark levels, multiplied by the unit cost of water and the production volume.

In addition to this quartile-one or best-in-class benchmarking approach, new digital technologies can drive performance beyond any existing benchmarks. It's the quartile-zero approach we reviewed in Chapter 3.

Not all gaps can be closed without CAPEX investment because of technological differences: old versus new machinery, ERPs versus legacy systems etc., so, the calculated savings should be adjusted to factor in these differences. The CAPEX investment and corresponding additional savings should then be put up for discussion in a specific business case. The sum of all monetized gaps assigned to each cost category forms the high-level savings targets in the next phase of value targeting: close the gap.

But company resources – time, money and talent – are limited. So

Savings Opportunity Prioritization Matrix

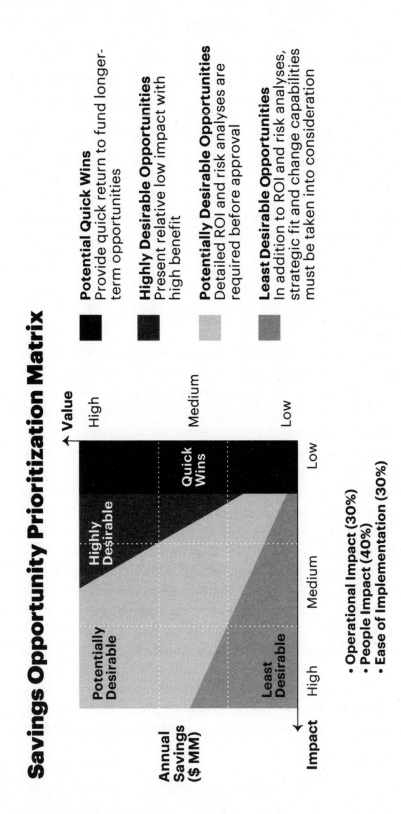

Value

High

Medium

Low

Annual Savings ($ MM)

Potentially Desirable

Highly Desirable

Quick Wins

Least Desirable

Impact

High   Medium   Low

- Operational Impact (30%)
- People Impact (40%)
- Ease of Implementation (30%)

Potential Quick Wins
Provide quick return to fund longer-term opportunities

Highly Desirable Opportunities
Present relative low impact with high benefit

Potentially Desirable Opportunities
Detailed ROI and risk analyses are required before approval

Least Desirable Opportunities
In addition to ROI and risk analyses, strategic fit and change capabilities must be taken into consideration

not all opportunities can be pursued by the company immediately, or at all. That means savings opportunities should be prioritized according to their potential value, ease of implementation and contract constraints.

To close the gap, an even more detailed look into the organization is required. Deeper discussions with subject-matter experts are an efficient way to identify and quantify initiatives. In these conversations, executives split into groups to cover cost categories. Each group can then analyse each department, understand ongoing improvement initiatives and evaluate best practices to be replicated elsewhere in the company.

Value targeting and revenues

Warren Buffett once said: 'The single most important decision in evaluating a business is pricing power. If you've got the power to raise prices without losing business to a competitor, you've got a very good business.'[2] The quote underscores why ZBx focuses so relentlessly on pricing. In ZBx, pricing is the biggest profit improvement lever, even more effective at boosting margins than increased sales or cost reduction.

In fact, the multiplier effect of optimizing pricing is enormous: for many companies, a 1 per cent price increase yields a 7 to 14 per cent improvement in operating profit,[3] while the impact of a similar improvement in fixed cost is five times smaller. What's more, in our experience, revenue optimization – of which pricing is a key element along with sales and channels and customer service – can deliver 1 to 3 per cent improvement (as a percentage of sales) in value for clients.

When ZBx is applied to pricing, a deep understanding of a company's current price-setting approach, as well as its price and cost structure, is gained, which enables the establishment of pricing and profitability baselines. With these baselines in mind, the company's pricing strategy, market positioning and operational performance are all evaluated to identify optimization areas: product- and customer-specific actions that serve as building blocks for a sustainable revenue optimization programme to drive top-line growth.

Clearly defining the pricing strategy and ownership of pricing decisions is a pivotal step on the path to optimization. That's why an accountability map is created to interlock the responsibilities between pricing decision-making and execution. Sales and commercial teams need to be educated so they're equipped to act on zero-based price-setting and discounting rules and respond in real time to market dynamics.

Value targeting and costs

Let's use a function many companies can relate to – the supply chain – to illustrate how value targeting works for costs. The supply chain costs of a manufacturing company can be decomposed according to its capabilities – plan, source, produce, package and move – and overhead.

The first step in any plan to open the gap is to load the network, footprint, inventory and order data into a business intelligence (BI) platform. This will enable us to understand plan levels, inventory levels, lead times and service levels. Next, benchmarking against operational and financial KPIs is conducted. Then maturity assessments against demand (activity and forecast), supply (network and inventory), S&OP (decision inputs and finance alignment) and general trends (segmentation, concurrent planning, move to short term) are executed.

The gap is closed by redefining the different segments, deploying the power of machine learning on demand planning and scheduling, using concurrent planning solutions as part of supply network planning, and adjusting S&OP to cover mid- and short-term execution.

The outcome: full visibility on planning maturity, cost and performance, internal and external benchmarks for plan performance, and an automation-based planning framework according to the specific client network and requirements.

Moving on to the source capability, a value-engineering approach is applied to leverage internal and external benchmarking. Detailed should-cost models and analytics are also used to identify cost-improvement opportunities. To open the gap, an overview of spend per region and product category is necessary. Then, specifications and stock-keeping unit (SKU) data are reviewed, and the supplier base for each SKU is analysed. Finally, internal benchmarking across different categories is conducted to identify first-quartile and best-in-class performance level, investigate quartile-zero* opportunities, create should-cost models and execute extensive cost modelling.

The gap is closed with the identification of opportunities to optimize material pricing across regions and suppliers. That includes a review of supplier contracts and additional opportunities, the assessment of impact (risk versus benefit), and the evaluation of sustainability benefits.

The outcome: a clear understanding of cost structure and drivers, visibility of end-to-end cost of execution per opportunity, components (or materials) and product price optimization, and the identification and communication of sustainable value.

For production costs, the approach involves reviewing cost and service-level drivers for plant productivity and assessing the automation potential. The gap is opened by contrasting productivity across plants, assessing the overall equipment effectiveness (OEE), identifying the impact of product subgroups on the complexity and cost of production and packaging processes, and identifying efficiency and value drivers by analysing global top performers.

The gap is closed by creating what-if models to identify the best scenario between cost and service levels. This involves assessing

---

* In a nutshell, quartile zero is forward-facing benchmarking. It does not measure a company against what others are doing today, but against how new digital technologies can be applied to shift your cost curves dramatically (see details in Chapter 3).

process-streamlining opportunities – optimizing batch sizing, organizational sizing, production planning and scheduling etc. – using predictive asset maintenance. Machine learning is leveraged to improve asset utilization and reduce downtime and maintenance costs. Finally, additional automation and digitalization initiatives are identified to improve performance.

The outcome: plant cost and performance heat maps, total plant throughput assessment, what-if models to make fact-based decisions between costs and service levels, and OEE improvement initiatives including automation and digitalization.

In packaging, value engineering is critical. The gap is opened by leveraging the visibility phase to prioritize focus areas, cost categories, product categories and geography. How? By reviewing specifications and SKU data and understanding the supplier base by SKU. Should-cost models are then built to find the ranges for savings by evaluating the portfolio of products from market, consumer and competitive perspectives. And comparing client versus competitor product specifications. Extensive cost modelling is used to identify quartile-zero cost-savings potential.

The gap is closed by optimizing product specs, standardizing parts and components, reducing weight, eliminating parts and features, and substituting materials. Insights are developed on components of product specifications that drive customer experience. For example, companies can use advanced analytics to assess positioning on customer experience versus costs, review opportunities with cross-functional teams (marketing, operations and supply chain), assess the potential impacts of opportunities, evaluate sustainability benefits and conduct consumer trials.

The outcome: an understanding of consumer requirements concerning product attributes, visibility of end-to-end cost of execution per opportunity, business case and bottom-up analysis per opportunity, a phased roadmap for implementation, product-spec optimization and sustainable value identification.

'ZBx creates the space for people to think differently and to take the sacred cows by the horns.'

– MULTINATIONAL RETAILER

Value targeting for the move capability is based on should-cost and scenario modelling, incorporating internal and external best practices and trends. The gap is opened with granular spend visibility per supplier, mode and region, analysis of warehouse rate cards and productivity, analysis of contract and performance management and detailed benchmark analysis.

The gap is closed with what-if scenario modelling including cost-to-serve and network modelling, a detailed cost-to-serve optimization considering business and brand-driven restrictions, and operational innovations such as advanced spot-buys for logistics and automation and robotization solutions for warehousing. This drives full visibility into logistics performance, should-cost modelling and what-if scenario modelling. The next diagram illustrates some of the what-if scenarios.

Lastly, there are overhead costs in the supply chain or the organization overall. Efforts surrounding overhead should focus on value-add activities, ensuring the 'five rights' are in place: right work, right size, right structure, right people and right measurement.

- **Right work** It's becoming clearer by the day: the work and routines of today aren't necessarily right for tomorrow. Focusing on the right work means focusing on the work that can be eliminated (what's not contributing to a valued outcome) as well as the work that's differentiated (and perhaps needs more investment).
- **Right size** Companies should identify how much work volume is coming through the system. They should ask:

LEVERS	KEY DRIVERS	OPPORTUNITY HYPOTHESIS

Net Price

Per Mile

Rate Negotiation — In addition to bi-annual freight bid, use TMS to continuously identify low cost rate options and spot bids

Mode Optimization — Opportunity to gain visibility around holistic multi-modal optimization for both inbound/outbound freight as well as freight consolidation

Dedicated Fleet — Shifting additional high frequency movements (i.e. shuttles) to a dedicated fleet vs. common carrier for cost-saving opportunities

Other Costs

SLAs / Contract Policies — Create and monitor policies governing carrier performance (e.g. on-time arrival, wait times, fleet characteristics, etc.), with real-time visibility

Payment Terms — Work with carriers to obtain discounts based on timing of payments to get credit for paying well w/in 30-day contractual agreement (pmt in 2–5 days)

Customer Segmentation — Segmenting customers based on priority transportation needs (i.e. OTIF, followed by rate, followed by schedule) to better serve

Internal Labour

Scheduling — • Define best practices with respect to scheduling and turning carriers at refineries to become shipper of choice
• Define the org and talent model to balance cost and desired service

Customer Service — • Reduce refinery internal labour by better scheduling and adherence to planned deliveries/pickups

Contract Management — Adjust contracts to help define and address capability gap to manage carrier base and adherence

Revenue Recognition

Freight Absorption — Segmented customer freight policies to enable company to recapture freight cost. Adherence to actual freight cost collection

Distance

Planning

Demand and Supply Plan — Build end-to-end planning capability to increase accuracy of available supply by node
Eliminate miles by shifting demand from refineries to closer locations where possible

Industry Capacity — Improve flexibility and awareness to industry trends to shift between modes quickly and efficiently

Utilization

Route Optimization — Internal or external capabilities to optimize routing to serve customer needs in the most cost-efficient way (distance, mode, equipment, etc.)

Network Design — Opportunity to eliminate miles from redundant/unnecessary movements and shift production based on regional demand

Asset Utilization — Increase utilization of each mode (e.g. loading policies and practices) and manage own fleet leasing (e.g. rail)
Reduce carrier time at or in a refinery to become shipper of choice

how much can be automated? How much could be changed by altering service-level agreements or company policy? How much can be resized (up or down, depending on value)?

- **Right structure** Organizational designs should be reconsidered. That means deciding the leadership, layers and span of control required to perform specific work activities. Importantly, the structure should only be set after understanding the right work and right size.
- **Right people** This is tied with right work – today's talent needs won't necessarily be suitable for tomorrow. Companies should consider changing skillsets and whether those new skills should be built or bought and at what cost.
- **Right measurement** Companies should measure themselves against the new picture of success developed courtesy of ZBx.

The gap is opened with a benchmarking exercise of the current headcount and labour productivity, a prime value chain study that creates a pragmatic end-to-end model to show how work gets done. This is followed by a big ideas workshop that defines the list of initiatives to unlock additional savings potential.

The gap is closed with the identification of value-add activities – 'where to invest' and 'where to optimize' – by function or region, including debottlenecking operations, harmonizing roles, applying wage arbitrage by centralizing roles, automating and digitizing activities, and transforming operating models to break down silos and streamline operations.

Establishing accountability

Over time, like the other capabilities within ZBx, value targeting becomes business-as-usual and is performed continuously to nail cost and revenue wins. With visibility established and targets set, the next capability to master is category ownership.

A zero-based mindset creates an unprecedented level of accountability to outcomes decided in the value targeting phase by creating a 'healthy tension' between category and entity owners. This tension expands and accelerates the potential to realize its ambition. More on that in the next chapter: category ownership.

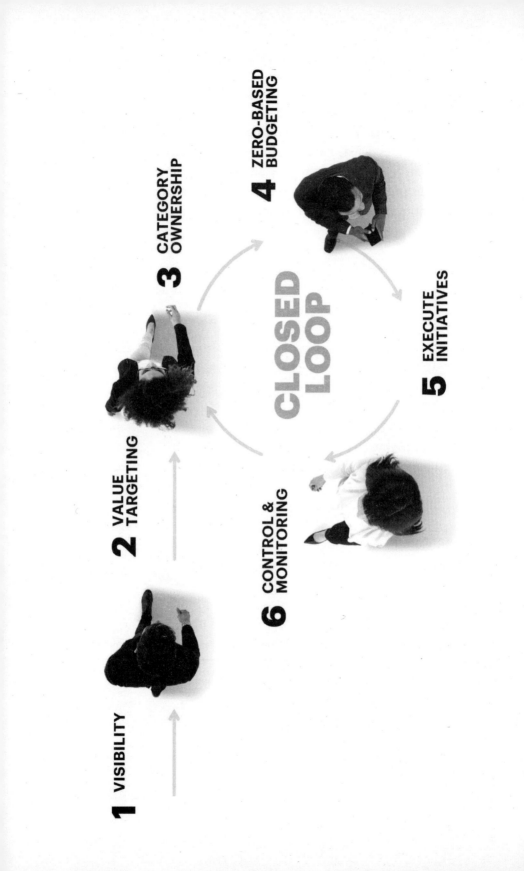

1 VISIBILITY

2 VALUE TARGETING

3 CATEGORY OWNERSHIP

4 ZERO-BASED BUDGETING

5 EXECUTE INITIATIVES

6 CONTROL & MONITORING

CLOSED LOOP

8. Category Ownership – Shining Light in the Darkest Corners

Have you ever crossed the street before a dark corner because you couldn't see what was in front of you? Shady things happen where no one can see. What if a lamppost illuminated your way, making the path ahead perfectly clear? ZBx is your company's floodlight, shedding clarity on all types of spend, leaving no stone unturned and no corner 'in the dark'. And category ownership establishes who controls the light switch and the direction of the beam.

Category ownership is a governance model that forges a shared responsibility between an entity/budget and cost category owners (see diagram on page 83). This pairing drives a dual perspective on each and every resource decision. And in the bargain, it creates a tension – a healthy one – that will define and sustain improvement and keep the engine of ZBx humming.

What are the qualities of a solid category owner? Try to find people who can be flexible in how they look at business conditions, with the curiosity to think about things in a different way. They need to be motivated to take risks. Within the organization there has to be a tolerance for risk at both the macro and micro levels to empower category owners to make decisions.

At the end of the day, this is just good management, right? Yet few companies fully leverage the power of category ownership to drive their ZBx journeys. That may be because the finance organization feel they're ceding some of their traditional territory to the category owners. But on the other hand, the function gains a new strategic role beyond the stewardship of a company's finances. Through category management, finance players become the coaches to colleagues who aren't necessarily 'numbers people'.

Now we can get into the details of the three pillars of category ownership.

Entities and entity owners

Again, entities are the lowest-level units for which budgets are created and then monitored. The golden rule for them: they must have a unique manager with the authority to establish priorities and prepare budgets for all activities and personnel within the entity. And they need the corresponding responsibility to deliver by controlling revenues (by changing prices, reducing or creating SKUs) and spend (by stopping purchases, reducing headcount). The managers of each entity are called entity owners. Entity owners are still responsible for managing their P&L but they also:

- **Annually** Own all revenue and expense within the entity and know their entity's spend requirements. They understand and adopt the established standards, rules and guidelines while preparing and spending their budgets.
- **Monthly** Track and monitor entity expenses, understand variances at a granular level and develop and implement corrective action plans to meet targets in the next month.
- **Daily** Drive entity compliance with standards and guidelines, approve or deny unbudgeted expenses and look for new ways to save.

Sometimes, companies are tempted to cascade budgets down from entity level to responsibility-centre level. Cascading isn't necessary or recommended since additional time and effort must be spent not only by the entities and cost category owners at budget preparation, but also by everyone else in the organization during weekly and monthly monitoring if incorrect postings to responsibility centres arise. When spending is incorrectly allocated in several responsibility centres and accounts, the number of corrections and the associated cost magnify quickly. Less data can actually be more meaningful data.

CATEGORY OWNER

ENTITY OWNER

	Operations	Finance	Real Estate	Marketing	IT	HR

Travel

Facilities

Compensation & Benefits

Financial Services

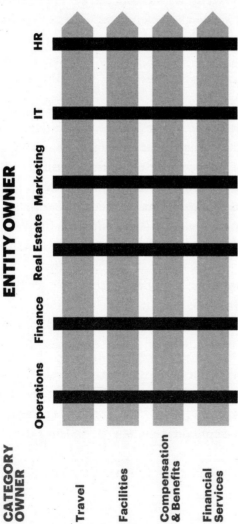

CATEGORY OWNERS

- Have a deep understanding of cost drivers (price and consumption)
- Establish and ensure compliance with policies for cost category and subcategories
- Challenge budgets across all departments for the specific category
- Identify and spread best practices
- Identify opportunities and validate action plan
- Validate cost category budget
- Monitor/control cost category expenses (actual vs. budget)

PROFILE

- Senior
- Knowledgeable on company
- Ready to 'lead by example'

ENTITY OWNERS
(Budget Owner)

- Responsible for budgeting and monitoring their cost centre budgets
- Use the guidelines and policies and work with cost category owners to prepare their budgets
- Negotiate and validate budget with each cost category owner

Cost categories

Cost categories are the aggregate of accounts of a similar nature and theme within a general ledger, of material size to the organization, and that usually (but not always) are common to several entities. They drive forensically detailed and standardized visibility into an organization's spending and are used to account for and control the use of resources.

Each category is assigned to a senior executive who will act as category owner. These executives serve as the ZBx champions in the organization. They shape and defend guidelines that may not be popular with management since they reduce access to a company's unofficial benefits such as company cars. Category owners will gain a new set of responsibilities, often in addition to their day job:

- **Annually** Understand the nature of the spend in their categories and define or update category standards and budget guidelines. They do everything from setting budget targets to enforcing adherence to key policies.
- **Monthly** Review actual performance compared with budget and work with entity owners to understand variances. This encompasses things like taking corrective actions to reduce overrun and sharing best practices.
- **Daily** Monitor compliance to approved standards, rules and guidelines as budgeted resources are used. Review and approve purchase orders for the category and answer questions on how to handle unbudgeted expenses.

Beyond being flexible, something we mentioned at the beginning of this chapter, category owners need a deep understanding of spend in their wheelhouse, and must be both senior enough to be tough on compliance and confident enough to challenge the status quo and drive change.

If deemed necessary by the category owner, they may be assisted by a category manager at certain stages of the ZBx process involving number-crunching and legwork. Category managers need to be knowledgeable of the accounts mapped to their category and have a good rapport with the category owner. Because category owners and managers are crucial to the success of ZBx, the right mix of will and skill is paramount. As a consequence, they must be picked from among the best and most committed people in the organization.

Category managers should not formally report to category owners in their business-as-usual activities or be responsible for major purchasing decisions within their category. An example: for IT spend, if the category owner is the CIO, then the manager could be someone from finance or operations who's able to challenge decisions from a user perspective. On the other hand, if the category owner is the CFO or from operations, then the manager should be someone from IT who will bring domain knowledge to complement the user point of view. In other words: avoid pairings from the same function, there's less tension and challenge.

Category managers and owners document and maintain everything from standards to best practices in the category definition books. A category definition book should provide:

- a detailed and standard definition of each account to enable consistent mapping of the company's cost structure;
- guidance as to what, how and by whom each expenditure may be budgeted, including the benchmark and budget guideline levels for that expenditure; and
- how and by whom each budgeted expenditure may be spent.

The category definition book should be read by entity owners, category owners and all other individuals involved in the ZBx process before they prepare their own budgets and whenever in doubt about how to post an expenditure in the general ledger.

Depending on specific circumstances, there could be additional category-ownership dynamics. In large, diverse or geographically dispersed organizations, different types of category owner systems might be enforced:

- **A two-tiered system** This is where a global category owner defines global guidelines and oversees the work performed by division or geography-specific category owners.
- **A deputy system** When there is a large number of entities, category deputies can act as intermediaries (span-breakers) between a group of entities and the category owner so that there are fewer but more effective interactions between the category owners and the entity owners.
- **A sponsorship system** Category sponsors (C-suite executives) can also be used to enforce compliance. They will choose the team (including the category owners), set the tone and ambition level and make tough decisions on behalf of the C-suite.
- **A co-ownership system** Procurement category co-owners are assigned to support the category owner. With this approach, an alignment of procurement categories with cost categories is required.

Matrix governance model

The matrix nature of the category-ownership model drives a 'checks and balances' governance dynamic through three principles:

- **Shared responsibility** The budget is prepared and monitored so that two people are simultaneously held accountable – the entity owner and the cost category owner.
- **Compliance to category budgeting guidelines** In every intersection, the corresponding entity must comply with the specific rules of the corresponding cost category. All

exceptions should be discussed and agreed to in advance of the publication of budgeting guidelines.

- **Budget ring-fencing** Budget in any intersection can be used only by that specific combination of entity and cost category. Hold the line when it comes to transfers between different categories or entities. Eliminate communicating vessels.

The matrix budget model creates a positive tension between category and budget/entity owners, and sparks teamwork around budgetary goals.[1] Since owners of cost categories and entities share responsibilities and are accountable for each intersection, this matrix model fosters discussions directed at challenging the use of resources. It also creates a double checking of expenditures: increasing budget visibility, improving expenditure monitoring and maximizing savings.

How? After a budget is approved, ring-fencing is in effect and there can be no compensation between categories. Before approval, entity owners can discuss goals with decision category owners and still make the necessary trade-offs among expense items and categories. They can, for example, decide to spend more money training the workforce to spot recycling opportunities to reduce maintenance materials costs. Subsequently, all communication between vessels is blocked.

Incentives

The right incentives need to be in place to encourage and recognize efforts, and ensure key players follow through with ZBx. Yet different people have different motivators: some are driven by more formal tangible incentives such as promotion, or bonuses to reward extraordinary outcomes, others by more intrinsic informal rewards such as greater authority, a sense of project ownership or the ensuing publicity of its success. Bonus triggers for category owners and managers should be different from those established for entity owners to reflect a higher level of time committed to zero-based mindset implementation.

Category owners and managers will add most value in the value-targeting and budget-preparation stages. So around 70 per cent of the ZBx bonus should be linked to the approval of the category budget by top management and the remaining 30 per cent to the end-of-year compliance to the approved budget. On the other hand, entity owners' main responsibility is to control their resources to be within the limits of the approved budget, so their ZBx bonus should be 100 per cent contingent to such compliance by year-end.

Since ZBx adds workload to the finance team and, in general, they will not benefit from the incentives offered, some companies devise one-time-only bonuses for them. Others use 'softer' motivation like singing the praises of these team members in internal newsletters, investing strongly in their career development, or offering leadership opportunities when appropriate.

Time to operationalize

At this point in a ZBx journey, the baselines are set and so are the ambitions. The necessary teams are ready to roll. Now it's time to operationalize by locking targets into a budget, the subject of our next chapter.

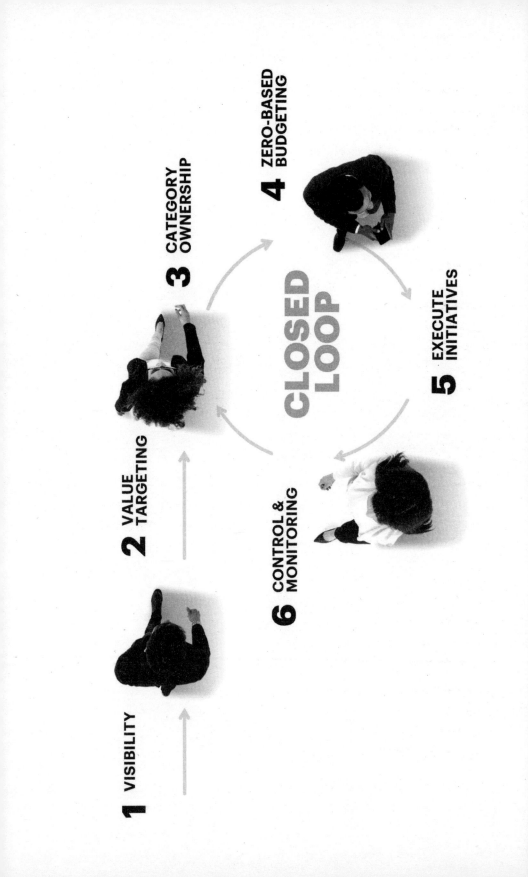

1 VISIBILITY

2 VALUE TARGETING

3 CATEGORY OWNERSHIP

4 ZERO-BASED BUDGETING

5 EXECUTE INITIATIVES

6 CONTROL & MONITORING

CLOSED LOOP

9. Lock Targets into the Budget – Promises, Promises

In a zero-based organization, budgeting isn't just about numbers. It's also about promises. Ones that won't be forgotten by the next quarter's review meeting. Because, through ZBx, targets are committed to, locked in and revisited. Again and again. This has the effect of making budgeting its own mini change programme within ZBx, creating a mechanism to get the entire organization pulling on the same oar and propelling the zero-based mindset forward towards meeting the strategic goals of the organization. This is achieved by:

- **Planning** Operational budgets are plans to deliver on the strategy and provide details of what management hopes to accomplish and how.
- **Motivation** Management can use operational budgets to motivate people to achieve the organization's overall objectives by committing them to a predetermined plan of action.
- **Evaluation** The data in an operational budget serves as a standard to compare a manager's or a business unit's actual results.
- **Coordination** When combined with the financial budgets into an overall master budget, operational budgets help coordinate activities by providing a consolidated plan of action.
- **Ownership** To prepare their budgets properly, managers at all levels of the organization must take a systematic and rigorous look at how their part of the business functions, and be aware of the behaviour of costs and revenues in their units.

In effect, a ZBx budget connects top-down ambition with bottom-up and tactical initiatives creating an encompassing culture of ownership throughout the organization. Other goodies it delivers are:

- **Transparency** Creates unprecedented spend visibility into key budget assumptions and where spend is earmarked.
- **Standardization** Drives consistency of the budgeting process and standards across the entire organization.
- **Accountability** Locks in the joint ownership of budgets, challenging entity owners to behave like owners of the company. And encouraging everyone to treat the company's money as their own.
- **Efficiency** Focuses on the 'need' for spending, rather than building on history.

At its core, ZBx is about agility – and getting companies to run in a more cost-efficient way to make them more competitive. Companies need to focus on their core strategic goals. Funds that don't work toward those goals (non-working money) should be shifted into activities that drive growth (working money). So budgeting non-working money should truly start from scratch – theoretically budgets should be zero-based, but for regulatory and other specific reasons like risk management, they are not. On the other hand, working money gets budgeted with outcomes and ROI in mind.

Let's take commercial spend, which is the investment that goes into creating customer demand. It includes sales, marketing, service, trade and promotional investment in the customer.

To maximize the return on the next incremental dollar, a portfolio investment allocation analysis is required. ROI analyses estimate the return from incremental spend.

Base and incremental ROI is assessed for each brand or product in the portfolio to achieve the optimal mix. ROI observations are then assessed in context with product life stage. Because newly launched products will typically have a different marketing mix

From non-working (bad costs) to working (good costs) money

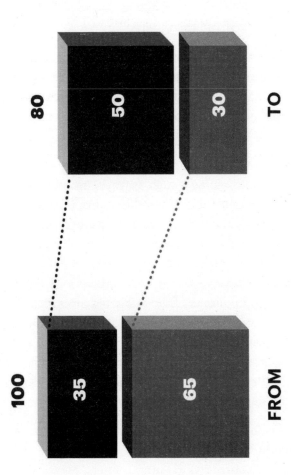

100   80

35   50

65   30

FROM   TO

and ROI profile from more established ones, long-term benefit must be considered. Finally, ROI and market attractiveness provide guidance for portfolio investment decisions. Product category risk factors (size, growth, competitive landscape) are assessed relative to ROI to develop strategic investment profiles.

To achieve the right balance between working and non-working money, a bottom-up approach is combined with traditional top-down budgeting and then merged into a consolidated plan:

- **Bottom-up budgeting (activity/FTE × payroll cost for ZBO, and price × quantity by cost/revenue component for ZBS, ZBSC and ZBC)** For the priority categories – based on value targeting scope – a bottom-up zero-based budget is developed with:

  - a predefined driver-based (FTE × Payroll or P × Q) methodology, such as travel (number of trips × average tariff × number of travellers), allowing budget owners to plan consumption/headcount while procurement and HR provide price/payroll expectation and productivity levers, or
  - descriptive (itemized) methodology detailing the components of the budgeted amount, such as consulting (e.g. by type of service, vendor, project/initiative, location, etc.), or
  - total spend (lump sum) methodology for when itemized detail is not required, such as office supplies (e.g. $300/month).

- **Top-down budgeting (baseline + inflation − productivity)** For the remaining categories, a top-down target is cascaded to entity owners. Productivity savings are informed through the outputs of the value targeting exercise.

Six enablers drive standardization and compliance to the ZBx methodology:

- **Category definitions book** An exhaustive revenue/spend guide that helps to drive the right scope.
- **Policies, standards and guidelines** Smart-spending policies, standards and guidelines to support a sustainable cost culture.
- **Budgeting guidelines** Detailed budgeting guidance designed to assist executives with issues like exchange, interest, GDP growth rates, etc.
- **Master data** Master data inputs that are used with the budgeting tools below (procurement master data, cost centres, etc.).
- **Targets** Targets that are available to guide the budgeting effort.
- **Budgeting tools** Customized tools and templates to facilitate the process.

The budgeting process consists of five phases: simulation, recommendation, review, negotiation and results measurement.

Budget simulation

The appropriate team simulates the next period's budget using the approved guidelines along with actual information from each entity (sales, production, headcount, etc.) to estimate a recommended budget and the corresponding savings. Besides reducing the timeframe of the budgeting process, this approach improves the chance of a successful implementation, especially in the first year, since entity owners will receive a recommended budget that:

- has been prepared to the adequate level of detail for the organization, so entity owners don't need to do the usual cascading/drilling down of corporate targets to their own entities;
- incorporates the guidelines defined for each intersection of entity and cost category, so the entity owner needs only to

understand the rationale behind the assigned guidelines and discuss the exceptions; and

- has been pre-approved by the category owners and the executive committee, so the usual budget negotiation rounds may eventually be non-existent to entity owners that accept it as is.

The simulation of the next period's budget can use a variety of tools: parametric modelling, bottom-up estimating and digital. Parametric modelling is enforced when benchmarks and guidelines have been defined. The approach involves using the efficiency guidelines in a mathematical model to predict the budget and corresponding cost savings. Models may be simple (a certain cost may be estimated using a single indicator, such as spend per mobile phone, employee, square foot of office space, etc.) or complex (using several adjustment factors, such as sales and marketing). Both the cost and accuracy of parametric models vary widely.

For most parametric modelling estimations, there are two types of costing:

- **Centrally allocated** This method is common when costs have a stepwise relationship to driver volume. So, if one entity adds a few more employees, it doesn't necessitate the renting of new space. But if all entities increase headcount, a decision to increase office space is a budgeting decision to be made centrally. If rent is allocated to different entities based on headcount, individual entity owners should not have to budget for rent. The rent for the entire budget should be accounted for centrally – usually from an agreed-upon contract, and the individual allocations calculated based on budgeted headcount.
- **Volume × rate costing** This is the method to use when there is a linear relationship between driver volume and costs. For example, adding a few employees will probably result in an increase in telephone costs. An entity owner would not budget for telephone costs – a rate per employee

would be applied to headcount budgeted earlier. This rate will be the defined guideline, which the entity owner may be empowered to edit at a later stage.

Bottom-up estimating is used for activities that cannot be associated with a driver and have usually gone through zero-base review. This technique involves estimating the cost of individual activities or business cases, then summarizing or rolling up the individual estimates to get an entity total. The cost and accuracy of bottom-up estimating is driven by the size and complexity of the individual activity or business case: smaller activities increase both cost and accuracy of the estimating process. The appropriate team should weigh the additional accuracy against the additional cost.

Digital tools such as budget simulation (e.g. Anaplan, IBM Cognos or Oracle Hyperion) or proprietary systems from consulting firms (e.g. Accenture's Aurora), are also widely used to assist with budget estimations. These products simplify the use of the tools described earlier and facilitate rapid consideration of alternatives. Regardless of which tool is chosen, supporting detail for the budget estimates must always be documented (even if only as rough notes), as they may prove valuable at the budget negotiation phase.

Budget recommendation

After the simulation is finished, the budget and underlying assumptions must be presented by the category owners to the executive committee and approved before it is communicated to entity owners. This step is necessary to attain the executive committee's buy-in and anchor the simulated results, encouraging them to champion and pursue such figures within their own organizations throughout the rest of the budgeting process.

Budget review

After entity owners have thoroughly reviewed their budget dossier, they are able to understand the budget that was recommended to them and identify exceptions. Such exceptions may be different targets, different pace to attain the targets, different cash flow, etc. Zero-based budgeting is a participative process and the more the entity owners discuss it with the relevant team and category owners, the bigger their buy-in and understanding of their own budgets.

At this point in time, entity owners will want to apply different budgeting techniques for different areas of the chart of accounts. Consider, for example, employee costs. Category owners are responsible for applying payroll tax rates in a centralized manner while entity owners will have to make decisions that differ between current and new employees. For existing employees, they can download a list of employees and their annual salary and other attributes from the general ledger or HR systems. They need to answer questions like:

- When will they get a raise?
- How big will the raise be?
- What tax rates should be applied to their salary?
- When and by how much will their benefits change?[1]

On the other hand, for new employees, there are additional questions:

- What month will they join?
- What is their annual salary?
- What will be their benefits?[2]

Similar situations apply to other accounts. Most, if not all, purchase prices and payment terms will be defined centrally by procurement and category owners, while entity owners will decide the purchase volume (or amount) and period.

Budget negotiation

After all entities propose their reviewed budgets, category owners must identify and understand the variations between the simulated budget recommended by them and the reviewed budget proposed by the entity owners. Differences usually fall into these categories:

- **Inflation** This variation occurs when entity owners apply inflation assumptions that are different from those originally published by the team.
- **Volume change** This variation occurs when entity owners apply volume assumptions, such as production, sale and/or distribution volumes, that are different from those originally published by the team.
- **Perimeter change** This variation occurs when entity owners apply perimeter assumptions, such as product lines, markets, channels etc., that are different from those originally published by the team.
- **New events** This variation occurs when entity owners budget new events, such as new acquisitions or divestitures, new regulations, special projects etc., that were not known or not predicted by the appropriate team, and therefore are not covered by the budget guidelines. New events are usually linked to strategic initiatives.
- **Pacing** This variation occurs when entity owners apply pacing assumptions for the capture of savings that are different from those originally predicted by the category owners.
- **Offences** This variation occurs when entity owners don't follow the guidelines.

The category owners should thoroughly understand the rationale behind the different assumptions about inflation, volume, perimeter, new events and phasing of results. Should the entity owners successfully prove the correctness of their assumptions, then the category owners must rewrite the category definitions book to include new guidelines addressing such assumptions. Otherwise, entity owners should rebudget according to the guidelines.

Offences must also be understood, but should not be accepted by the team. These have two main sources:

- **Budget proposed above the established guidelines** This derives from a misunderstanding of the guidelines or the ZBx principles and is easily corrected with the intervention of category owners.
- **Budget proposed above the adjusted baseline** This assumes a lower productivity than the status quo, going against every principle of the zero-based mindset. For some companies, that can lead to termination, since it demonstrates an unacceptable resistance to change by the entity owner. Other organizations may be more lenient. In any event, there should be consequences for ignoring the changes represented by ZBx.

All negotiation discussions must have their minutes shared among participants and all agreed adjustments to the budgets must be documented to avoid misunderstandings. It is essential that all parties agree to the negotiated budget and that entity owners and category owners are jointly accountable for the final figures.

Once all discussions have been finalized among entity owners and category owners, the final negotiated budget is consolidated and approved by the executive committee. The category owners are responsible for presenting it.

Budget results measurement

A budget prepared using the ZBx process is similar in format to that prepared in the traditional way, since all breakdowns must be entered into the organization's existing budget system for final approval and continuous monitoring of results. Documentation produced so far, including anything used to establish the benchmarks and guidelines, must be duly catalogued during budget closure. A complete set of indexed records should be archived and any pertinent historical databases updated.

Implementation plans have different timeframes for each category. Some, such as travel and mobile phones, are quick to implement and savings are captured immediately. Others may require renegotiation of contracts and will take longer. Phasing results will follow the same timeframes it takes for an expenditure level to reach the budget level.

From ambition to execution

With targets locked into the budget, and everyone in the organization living up to their promises, our next chapter will explore the linkage between the ambition of value targeting and the operationalization of budgeting through the execution of initiatives.

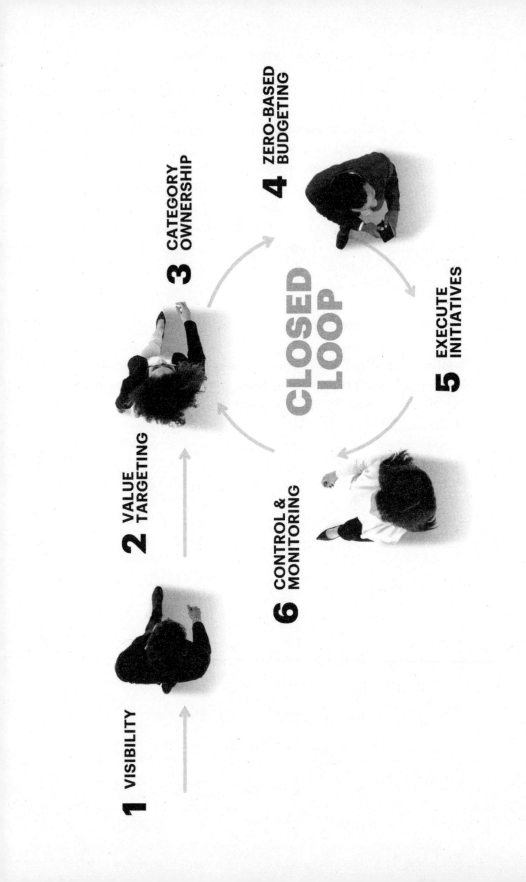

1 VISIBILITY

2 VALUE TARGETING

3 CATEGORY OWNERSHIP

4 ZERO-BASED BUDGETING

5 EXECUTE INITIATIVES

6 CONTROL & MONITORING

CLOSED LOOP

10. Execute Initiatives – from Theory to Action

Heads up: This is the most tactical and arguably the most difficult capability within the closed loop. Executing initiatives is all about ensuring ZBx moves from theory to action, bringing targets on a spreadsheet to life through real actions that shift behaviours. The right savings initiatives in policies, processes, people, technology and pricing will generate actual value that will in turn translate into sustainable results in the P&L.

A single company can have thousands of initiatives, each one aimed at closing the gap between the current and desired states, making sure that culture and behaviour changes are implemented and that the company continues to generate new ideas and further savings. Consider a global consumer goods company that used zero-based spending (ZBS) to free its capacity to fuel growth. The company saved $350 million in SG&A expenses in the first fiscal year of the programme and forecasts savings of $1.1 billion over three years. It enjoyed three consecutive quarters of adjusted margin expansion, with adjusted operating income margin up 140 basis points to 13.6 per cent in the third quarter. Improved margins helped them step up investment in production facilities, with new plants in Asia and an expansion of factories in Europe and the United States.[1]

Because ZBx initiatives include a wide range of interventions, and each company will have specific ground to cover, it's impossible to explore all of the possibilities thoroughly. Instead, we'll highlight examples of initiatives that illustrate the diversity of possibilities and propose a framework to help generate ones specific to your company's needs.

Let's start with zero-based organization (ZBO). In this phase, the outcome of ZBO would be an operating model aligned with the company's growth strategy and business model. That means first considering the strategy – what the company aspires to be in the future – and then the unique capabilities needed, and the work that must be performed, to turn that aspiration into a reality. It's about shifting resources to build the talent and capabilities in areas that are key to the company's ability to grow.

Take cable operators. Ten years ago, they were in the business of installation. Now they're in the business of delivering digital content. So, they need fewer network operators and more creative talent. Their new imperative is to model the best way to shift investment from the former to the latter.

But ZBO is also helpful in less-dire situations. Consider a manufacturer that wants to invest in emerging markets or ecommerce, for example. How could ZBO help it change to optimize its global sales and marketing spend? Most likely it would have grouped its global markets by proximity, but in doing so it could have overinvested in the wrong countries simply because they happened to be in the same geographic bucket as its stronger markets.

ZBO could be used to create archetypes for each country based on factors such as customer complexity, customer type and route to market. The result would be a new set of groupings, each sharing the same customer and market characteristics but not necessarily the same geography. This would enable the company to see where it was overinvesting in mature, low-margin markets and where it was underinvesting in growing markets, and ultimately to reallocate its sales and marketing resources.

Through zero-based supply chain (ZBSC), one client – a $25 billion-plus consumer goods company with more than a hundred manufacturing locations producing beverages for customers all over the world – found that raw materials, packaging and conversion costs made up approximately 44 per cent of their revenue. They set procurement, supply-chain and manufacturing strategies and budgets from a zero base, leveraging digital solutions such as machine learning, intelligent automation and control, and digital energy and safety management. The result: an initial drop of COGS to about 38 per cent.[2]

Digital technologies are also changing the game in the front office (ZBC). In the process, they're driving down costs. Advances in artificial intelligence have made chatbot interactions with customers commonplace. AI helps the chatbot anticipate customer questions, and if it doesn't have the answer, it can seamlessly transfer the interaction to a human agent. It's a virtuous circle: the costs saved by having fewer service reps are reinvested in the AI technology, which becomes ever more sophisticated until it can answer every question and drastically reduce the need for call centres entirely.

Using ZBC to attack pricing has paid off handsomely for many companies. Consider one utility operating in a high-competition, high-churn market. It found that its financial performance needed a boost. Customer economics identified a clear roadmap for change: the most profitable 7 per cent of customers drove the same value as the rest of the customer base. And the maximum value is twice as large as current total value. Armed with these insights, the utility defined a clear strategy for achieving a higher ROI on its digital investments, driving appropriate interventions to different profit segments. In the process, it increased its annual profit margin from its base customers by 15 per cent.[3]

In zero-based spend (ZBS), gap-closing initiatives will address both price and quantity of resources. They usually involve category owners, entity owners and procurement. Procurement deploys sourcing and purchasing initiatives to reduce unit costs, while category owners lead consumption-based initiatives and entity owners reduce spot and emergency purchases. Only by combining procurement, category owners' and entity owners' strengths will initiatives capture the forecasted results.

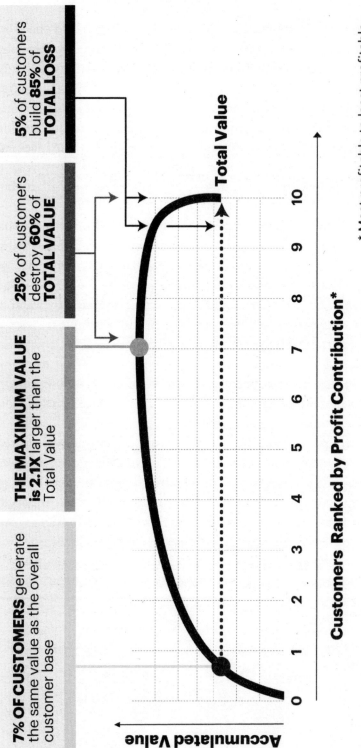

7% OF CUSTOMERS generate the same value as the overall customer base

THE MAXIMUM VALUE is 2.1X larger than the Total Value

25% of customers destroy **60%** of **TOTAL VALUE**

5% of customers build **85%** of **TOTAL LOSS**

Total Value

Accumulated Value

Customers Ranked by Profit Contribution*

* Most profitable to least profitable

SIDEBAR: What's procurement's role?

A procurement organization that follows the tenets of ZBx enforces standards and guidelines, channels demand and ensures compliance to achieve targeted savings. To secure the execution of ZBx initiatives, especially those linked to third-party spend, procurement and the associated source-to-pay processes play two main roles:

- Procurement negotiates or renegotiates deals with suppliers to enable new category consumption patterns. How? By securing goods and services compliant with new standards at a price that allows the organization to meet its budget.
- Procurement manages buying operations and ensures compliance to guidelines, policies and contracts. Digital procurement platforms and portals help channel users through the latest corporate standards. The end result: managers won't go 'rogue' on decisions, they will make the smartest purchases based on the insights gleaned from ZBx.

Let's look at how this works in reality: the sheer extension of facilities management contracts may not be fully understood by all users. So, users can be tempted to skip official channels and turn to local unauthorized suppliers instead. This increases the risk for bad service and for budget overruns of up to 50 per cent: a gap that's difficult to close. Digital procurement portals are a great way of providing easy access to certified suppliers and keeping budgets on target.

> *'ZBx moved us from a push to a pull model. We now get pulled by the executive committee. Before, we had to push our services.'*
>
> **– CPO OF A LIFE SCIENCES COMPANY**

Companies further down the road in their ZBx journey may want to dive into deeper waters by embracing a should-cost mindset (see Chapter 3). For example, by using digital workplace solutions such as smart building technologies, real-time operations management, space management and smart working, one company experienced a nearly 50 per cent drop in costs.[4]

From paper to profit

Simply generating and documenting initiatives is not enough. Another way to put that is 'Actions speak louder than words'. It's imperative to build an execution capability, otherwise the value of initiatives is only on sheets of paper, not the balance sheet. Each realm of ZBx may have a different yet complementary approach when it comes to executing initiatives. Let's compare two of them: ZBO and ZBS.

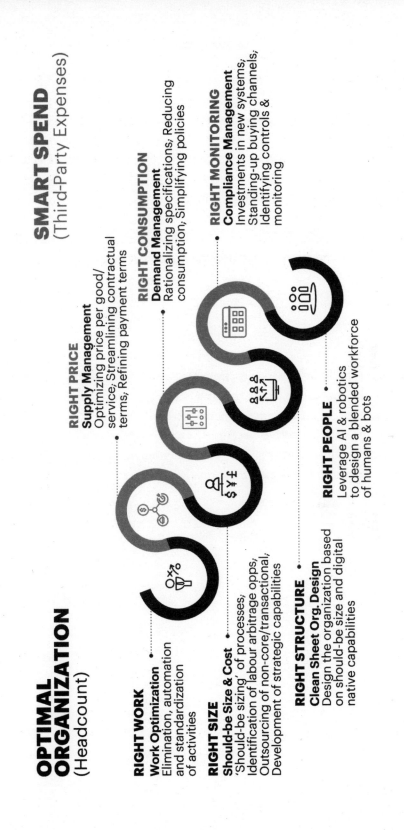

OPTIMAL ORGANIZATION
(Headcount)

RIGHT WORK
Work Optimization
Elimination, automation and standardization of activities

RIGHT SIZE
Should-be Size & Cost
'Should-be sizing' of processes; Identification of labour arbitrage opps; Outsourcing of non-core/transactional; Development of strategic capabilities

RIGHT STRUCTURE
Clean Sheet Org. Design
Design the organization based on should-be size and digital native capabilities

RIGHT PEOPLE
Leverage AI & robotics to design a blended workforce of humans & bots

SMART SPEND
(Third-Party Expenses)

RIGHT PRICE
Supply Management
Optimizing price per good/service; Streamlining contractual terms; Refining payment terms

RIGHT CONSUMPTION
Demand Management
Rationalizing specifications; Reducing consumption; Simplifying policies

RIGHT MONITORING
Compliance Management
Investments in new systems; Standing-up buying channels; Identifying controls & monitoring

While ZBO focuses on initiatives to deliver the right work, right size, right structure and right people, ZBS initiatives will deliver the right price, right consumption and right monitoring of third-party spend. As a result, a governance system should be in place to monitor the execution and address the interdependences between initiatives.

Early identification is often touted as the key to effective risk and cost management. Since initiatives hiccups often turn into small-scale actions on their own, early identification allows for better planning. And better planning means lower overall implementation costs.[5]

Making change stick

Consistent follow-through improves value realization and helps with the uptake of new pricing strategies and smart-spending guidelines. Monthly tracking enables the company to spend more time making proactive decisions, ensures the company meets its targets at the end of the year, and executes the growth opportunities identified. We'll elaborate on this in the next section: control and monitoring.

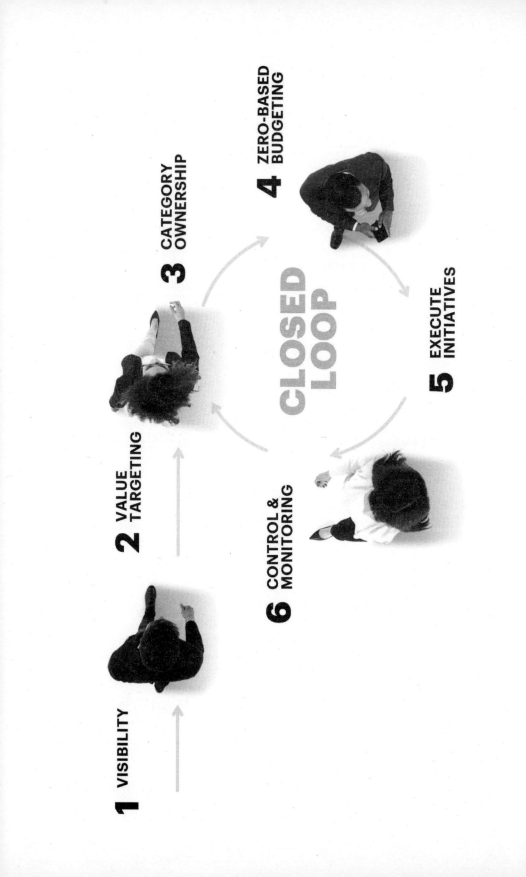

11. Control and Monitoring – Racing Ahead

Imagine yourself in a car on a race track. You've got a few clear goals. First, to win. But not at the risk of crashing. Second, to be bold enough to overtake competitors, but within the strategy agreed upon with your engineers. Lastly, to improvise. No one can predict all obstacles on the course. Consult your onboard display to monitor both the track and the status of your car, and take corrective action when required.

Driving ZBx in your organization is similar. You want to be the best. Visibility and value targeting show you where to go. You strive to go beyond the best-in-class. Quartile zero will lead you there. Category owners lay the guardrails and floor markings to show the way – the smart-spending guidelines. A healthy tension is created between cost category and entity owners as they lock the strategy into the budget.

Control and monitoring is about looking at past obstacles, assessing the current state and forecasting the future. It's also about improvising corrective actions to achieve the agreed budget if one runs off course. This is done through performance reporting and governance.

> *'ZBx moves the narrative from "give me x per cent of savings" to an activity-based conversation.'*
>
> – CFO OF AN OIL & GAS MULTINATIONAL

Performance reporting

Performance reporting has four main elements: variance analysis (actuals vs budget), understanding of root causes (operational KPIs), forecasting, and value management (tracking the progress of initiatives). These make explicit which budgets have been met and which have not, the underlying operational KPIs and the results of root-cause analysis. They also showcase the value generated by gap-closing initiatives and alert the ZBx team to issues that may cause problems in the future – i.e. the forecast. Often, AI tools are used to track budgeted costs versus actual costs, and to forecast the effects of volume and cost changes.

Reliable business intelligence (BI) and enterprise performance management (EPM) reports can be used to collect, filter, double-check and integrate data to report weekly and monthly results in a single format. This way, everyone is literally and figuratively 'on the same page'. It's the classic, 'single version of the truth'. This is essential to the longevity of a zero-based mindset. Without it, management will waste time discussing the accuracy of figures when they could be working out how to improve them.

A fixed monthly timeline for performance reporting is established by the team of category owners and agreed upon by the executive committee. Each organization should define its own timeline according to its capabilities and processes. A sample of one that's worked well for some companies is illustrated on the next page.

Let's look now at the four key mechanisms for perpetuating ZBx control and monitoring.

Variance analysis (actuals vs budget)

A critical part of control and monitoring lies in determining what causes budget variances and deciding whether the variance requires corrective action. Variance analysis enables managers to go beneath the surface of a reported difference between actual and expected

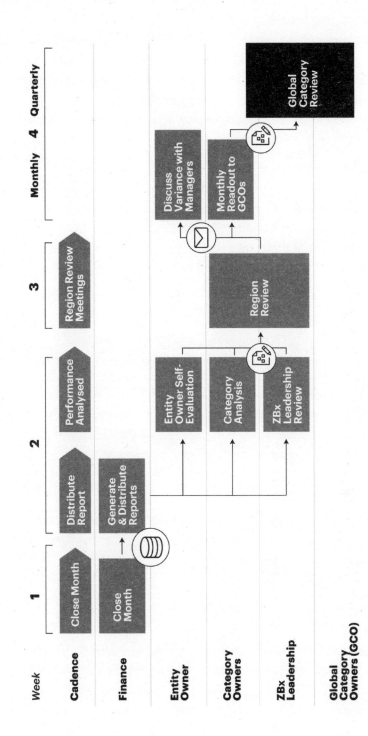

results, sharpening questions that can then be answered with further investigation.[1] The cause of variance, the reasoning behind the corrective action chosen, and other types of lessons learned should be documented and used in subsequent budget cycles.

Differences between budget and actual cost or revenue can be caused by:

- **Volume variance** Total sales or production volumes.
- **Mix variance** The mix of SKUs produced and distributed.
- **Price variance** Unit price of items purchased or sold.
- **Performance variance** Production norms and standards (e.g. ratio of input required to get one unit of output).
- **Currency variance** Related to trading in different markets with different currencies.

SIDEBAR: Variance formulas

Volume and mix variance $= (V_1 - V_2) \times P_1 \times N_1 \times C_1$

Performance variance $= V_2 \times P_1 \times (N_1 - N_2) \times C_1$

Price variance $= V_2 \times (P_1 - P_2) \times N_2 \times C_1$

Currency variance $= V_2 \times P_2 \times N_2 \times (C_1 - C_2)$

KEY

V = Volume produced (for supply and production costs)
  OR volume sold (for distribution costs and revenues)
P = Price (e.g. \$/kWh)
N = Norm (e.g. kWh/ton)
C = Currency exchange rate (according to market, e.g. \$/£)
1 = Baseline period (e.g. YTD or month budget)
2 = Most recent period (e.g. YTD or month actual)

The benefit from separating a variance into its different components is accountability, because different managers may be responsible for each component. Here's what we mean: the purchasing manager is responsible for buying materials at the budgeted price while the operations manager is responsible for using those materials efficiently (not using more than the budgeted quantity). The variance analysis shines a light on whether a material cost overrun is due more to purchasing behaviour than to operating inefficiencies or vice versa.

In practice, assigning responsibility is never quite so straightforward: a purchasing manager may acquire alternative materials and earn a favourable purchase price variance but the operations manager might then struggle to manufacture good enough products as a result. That could lead to more labour and machine time than budgeted, and an unfavourable performance variance. The question becomes: who's more responsible for the unfavourable efficiency variance – the operations manager or the purchasing manager?[2]

Under ZBx rules, a cost overrun or underrun is defined by a tolerance level. Only those variations that fall outside a certain tolerance level need to be explained and addressed by action plans. Tolerance levels reflect the accuracy of the budget and vary according to the nature of the category. So those categories with a reduced number of high-value postings (e.g. outsourced business support) or low predictability (e.g. travel), or that are subject to discretionary decisions (e.g. events and sponsorships) will have a higher tolerance. Proximity to year-end also plays an important part and zero tolerance is recommended in the last two months of the year to increase the likelihood of making budget.

Tolerance levels are necessary because, in extreme cases, use of the budget to force performance improvements may lead to a breakdown in corporate ethics. For example, people who worked at the now defunct telecom giant WorldCom reported that CEO Bernard Ebbers's rigid demands were an omnipresent stress that led to less-than-ethical behaviour. 'You would have a budget, and he would mandate that you had to be two per cent under budget,' noted one employee in an article in the *Financial Times*. 'Nothing else was acceptable.' WorldCom, Enron, Barings Bank and other failed companies had tight budgetary control processes that funnelled information only to those with a need to know.[3]

These breakdowns are more likely to occur as the pressure to improve performance increases, especially when economic conditions are deteriorating. Few CEOs want to miss their earnings targets and risk ridicule by investors and the media. And even fewer operating managers are willing to be upfront about bad news if it means incurring the wrath of superiors and forfeiting their bonus.

SIDEBAR: Ex-post-facto budget

There is a widely held belief that the objectives locked in a budget should be viewed as fixed standards against which performance will be judged. Let's assume, for example, there's a forecasted sales level of 4,000 units and a shipping cost of $25 per unit. This requires a shipping budget of $100,000. Let's then assume that the actual cost was $90,000 for 3,500 units. Where do we stand, variance wise? If you think there's a $10,000 cost underrun and that the leader of that unit should be rewarded, think again. That's because the company should have spent only $87,500 ($25 per unit times 3,500 units sold). Consequently, the company incurred a $2,500 overrun instead.

A flexible budgeting mindset preaches that output levels are usually external variables that should not impact the evaluation of a leader's performance, so it isolates the effects of changes in sales volume or production level from other performance factors.

For many companies, the most effective budget for evaluation purposes is an 'ex-post-facto' budget or, as it translates, a budget after the fact. Why? Because it is constructed or adjusted allowing for the impact of uncontrollable or unforeseeable events. Examples of expenses that might be deemed uncontrollable by an individual manager are allocations of corporate over-head such as leasing of facilities and IT infrastructure. Examples of unforeseeable impacts are gains or losses due to fluctuations in foreign exchange rates.

Let's illustrate this. Volume variance is generally consid-ered uncontrollable for operations managers, but these managers are held accountable for the efficiency vari-ance. The ex-post-facto budget identifies those expenses that the manager is expected to reduce when actual vol-umes are decreasing or, conversely, the expenses that can be increased when actual production exceeds the bud-geted capacity.[4]

As a consequence, in this mindset, the impact of produc-tion or sales volume changes would be accounted for before variation tolerance levels are applied in order to avoid false alarms (e.g. overruns due to increased produc-tion or underruns to budget due to reduced production). On variable categories, and some semi-variable categories, the most important indicators to be monitored are unit cost (e.g. cost per ton) and specific consumption or efficiency (e.g. tons of raw material or tons of product). Provided the entity has complied with established unit cost and specific consumption, they should not be required to explain variations. But for budget versus actual comparisons, a volume-adjusted virtual budget must be calculated.

Understanding of root causes (operational KPIs)

Based on the variances identified, entity owners will look at the operational KPIs for specific functions to understand their root cause (see diagram on next page).

The root cause analysis from the variance reports will result in clear actions to drive savings sustainability, with specific people in charge, and usually sponsored by category owners and senior executives.

Understanding operational KPIs also helps answer three important questions:

- Are achieved savings reflected in the P&L performance?
- How can I see what the KPI improvement costs me?
- What's the impact on my P&L if the target KPI drops below the budgeted level?

Forecasting

At the end of each month, entity owners not only are responsible for seeing that the actual results of operations are reported but should also provide a forecast for the portion of the overall budget period remaining. These revised forecasts become inputs to the planning process and serve to update those plans that were based on either the original budget or the most recent forecast.

The most common forecasting techniques are:

- **Actuals to date plus a new estimate for the remaining months** This approach is used when past performance shows that the original assumptions were fundamentally flawed, or that they are no longer relevant owing to a change in conditions.
- **Actuals to date plus remaining budget** This approach is most often used when current variances are seen as atypical and the management team expectations are that similar variances will not occur in the future.

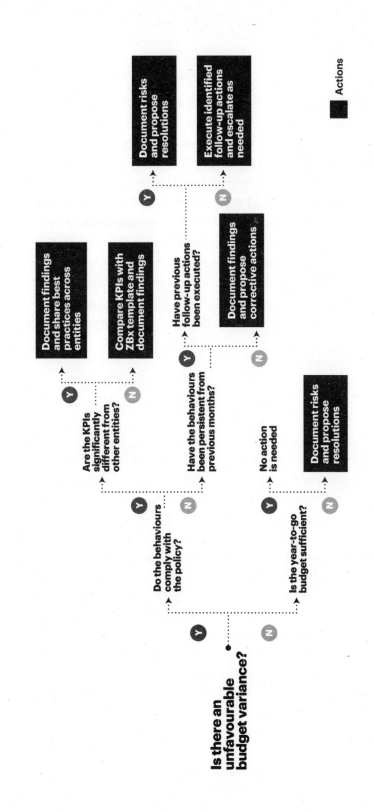

Is there an unfavourable budget variance?

Y → Do the behaviours comply with the policy?

Y → Are the KPIs significantly different from other entities?

Y → Document findings and share best practices across entities

N → Compare KPIs with ZBx template and document findings

N → Have the behaviours been persistent from previous months?

Y → Have previous follow-up actions been executed?

Y → Document risks and propose resolutions

N → Execute identified follow-up actions and escalate as needed

N → Document findings and propose corrective actions

N → Is the year-to-go budget sufficient?

Y → No action is needed

N → Document risks and propose resolutions

■ Actions

Value management

In the first year of ZBx implementation, a value-realization office (VRO) – or control tower – should be established to follow gap-closing initiatives and track and forecast value realization.

The VRO works with category owners and entity owners to monitor the execution of ongoing initiatives, verify the corresponding actual results in the P&L, investigate variances against value-realization targets and confirm upcoming value-realization forecasts.

New technologies combined with data science enable companies to get under the hood and continuously monitor these initiatives and corresponding results. This is especially important for ZBSC with its myriad of operational KPIs, and ZBO, since it's extremely hard to have real-time visibility on who does what at any point in time.

Governance

Governance of the control-and-monitoring process is driven by the interaction of categories and entities owners at different aggregation levels. For example, on a monthly basis, category owners will engage with the 20 per cent of entities causing 80 per cent of the variance to maintain the healthy tension established in the category-ownership phase. In global companies, there could be additional levels of interaction, for example involving regional and global category owners.

When confronted with variations between budget and actual spending, executives develop corrective action plans to improve their performance and, as a consequence, increase their chances of meeting the budget. The results of these interactions, along with the variances against the budget and corresponding action plans, are presented to the executive committee during monthly ZBx performance meetings.

These meetings are of paramount importance for fostering a new cost-management culture throughout the organization, and for ensuring everyone will be held accountable for their own results: good and bad. To reinforce the success story of ZBx internally, it's important to acknowledge standout performance. One idea: invite the entity owners with the best overall quarterly saving performance to present their best practices to the executive committee. Another: have the CEO visit the entity with the best quarterly results, giving them face time and recognition from the boss.

'Some people say that the monthly control-and-monitoring meetings involve a lot of people for a long period of time discussing small amounts and variances. But it's when you go through this discipline that you hit big fish.'

– CEO OF A CONSUMER GOODS COMPANY

Unleashing the future of digital finance[5]

We've so far discussed the present of ZBx control and monitoring. What's in its future?

Business leaders need daily sales and near-real-time profitability reporting to make the right decisions to drive growth and maintain business agility. It's a paradigm shift that moves finance away from a reporting function to one that puts information at the fingertips of executive leadership in near-real time. The pace of change is only getting faster. The new imperative for business is exponential growth. If the finance function moves too slowly when it comes to gaining bench strength through digitalization, then agility atrophies, as does growth.

To unlock the value of digitalization, CFOs must develop a comprehensive AI strategy as part of a broader digital road map. Companies can use machine learning to process, validate or correct journal entries at the time of booking. The same machine-learning capabilities can perform continuous reconciliations between systems, ledgers and intercompany transactions. This dramatically decreases the need for humans to perform time-consuming reconciliations, so the need for control testing largely disappears. Continuous accounting enables continuous cognitive auditing, accelerating the remaining tests to a real-time basis and ultimately enabling 'continuous close', leaving the days of closing books on a monthly or quarterly basis a remnant of an antiquated past.

Parting thoughts . . .

Several business books have become global best-sellers, claiming that a company can achieve success if it follows their specific set of steps. This is not one of them. We offer no miracles. No guarantees. No return policy. Sorry!

As we've highlighted in discussions about benchmarking and quartile zero, performance is relative. Success and failure depend not only on your actions but also on those of the other players in the market. It matters not where you are at the moment; a little where you're going; a lot how fast you're getting there. If rivals improve at a faster rate, you will be left behind. Game theory 101.

So, the zero-based mindset is neither a panacea nor a silver bullet, despite what its track record may show.[1] ZBx is a successful tried and true tool to continually improve efficiency and forever change cost culture in organizations. It is an ongoing process which companies are drawn to not just because they want to shrink this year's budget. It is not merely a matter of post-merger right-sizing or showing Wall Street how much value can be delivered at speed.

Companies that adopt ZBx are investing in it for the long haul. Because it provides a way of fundamentally reshifting resources to fund innovation and growth. Casting out bad – non-working – cost, while boosting good – working – cost and competitive agility. It is a new classic that drives benefits that speak for themselves as they help companies compete and grow.[2]

Different people will give different advice on how to achieve it. And there's no one-size-fits-all answer. But we believe that the closed-loop approach is the best cost-management toolkit out there. And we see three of its capabilities as non-negotiable for making ZBx durable:

- **Forensic visibility** that shifts organizational mindsets from perception to cold hard reality, creating a new lens to look at cost items and segregate good costs and bad costs.
- **Category ownership** – a new spend governance model that creates a healthy tension between different groups of people who are simultaneously accountable for every dollar spent.
- **Control and monitoring** that creates a virtuous cycle of self-reinforcing insight and action that constantly gauges how resources are allocated against strategic desire.

On the horiZon

So where are we heading with ZBx? On the near horizon we'll see an expanded adoption across the whole P&L. It has already burst out of the confinements of SG&A – zero-based spend (ZBS) – and into the domain of the other baby Zs: zero-based organization (ZBO), zero-based commercial (ZBC) and zero-based supply chain (ZBSC).

On a longer timeline, AI and machine learning will continue to accelerate the capabilities that underpin the approach as they become even more adroit at pinpointing areas of trapped value. As we continue to harness information and automate it, among the game changers on the horizon are developments like 'touchless budgeting'. That's where a rich stream of data can be wielded to produce budget simulations – instantly and accurately – to project any number of realities.

Technology will also ameliorate closed-loop routines, making them faster and more flexible. Enhancements within (ERP) systems in the area of in-memory calculation will make the routines and interactions with everybody in the company more immediate, with root-cause analysis at your fingertips now, not at the end of the month, and providing alerts on budget impact before cost is committed to. Thinking about upgrading your ERP? S/4HANA anyone? You may want to design the new routines and data models with ZBx in mind. Technological innovation will also increase transparency internally and, in an ever more connected world, externally. The result: more initiatives that are good for society and the trust equation of organizations.

One last thought

The momentum around ZBx today mirrors the early years of digital transformation. First movers ignored the sceptics and went 'all-in' on digital. Some wound up reinventing business models, customer experiences and even entire industries in the process. The buzz reached a fever pitch, and laggards followed suit. Flash forward to today, and companies that are behind in digital are behind competitively. Digital has become non-negotiable for survival.

Soon, the same will be said for ZBx.

References

Accenture (2015a), *Structural Cost Transformation & Enabling the Growth Agenda Survey*. Accenture

———(2015b), *ZBB and Closed-Loop Cost Management: An Engine for Growth*. Accenture

———(2016a), *Accenture Acquires Realworld OO Systems B.V., a Leading Utilities Geographic Information System Business*. Accenture

———(2016b), *Accenture AS Operations Insights and Future of Procurement Study*

Accenture Strategy (2016a), *Fueling Growth Through Zero-Based Budgeting: How Winners Know Where to Place Big Bets*. Accenture Strategy

———(2016b), *Memo to the C-Suite: You are Not the Main Driver of Change*. Accenture Strategy

———(2017), *HR/Employee Experience Study*. Accenture Strategy

Andrews, K. (2018), *ZBx? Get Serious (About Culture Change)*. Accenture Strategy

Askew, K. (2016), Why Zero-Based Budgeting is Shaking Up the Food Sector. *Just-Food*, 6 October

Babcock, C. (2016), GE Doubles Down on 'Digital Twins' for Business Knowledge. *Information Week*, 24 October

Barea, D., Banerjee, S., Feliciano, P. and Mueller, J. (2017), *Smart Spending is Not Just About the Numbers*. Accenture Strategy

Bhatt, M. (2018), *From Back (Office) to the Future*. Accenture Strategy

ConAgra Foods, Inc. (2015), ConAgra Foods Announces $300 Million Efficiency Plan, Establishes Chicago Headquarters. www.conagrabrands. com/news-room/news-conagra-foods-announces-300-million-efficien cy-plan-establishes-chicago-headquarters-2092152

Corr, A. (2018), *Is Your Supply Chain in a Death Spiral?* Accenture Strategy

Correa, C. (2014), *Dream Big: How the Brazilian Trio Behind 3G Capital – Jorge Paulo Lemann, Marcel Telles and Beto Sicupira – Acquired Anheuser-Busch, Burger King and Heinz*. Sextante

Daneshkhu, S., Whipp, L. and Fontanella-Khan, J. (2017), The Lean and Mean Approach of 3G Capital. *Financial Times*, 7 May

Daugherty, P., Banerjee, P., Negm, W. and Alter, A. E. (2015), *Driving Unconventional Growth Through the Industrial Internet of Things*. Accenture

Daugherty, P. and Wilson, H. J. (2018), *Human + Machine: Reimagining Work in the Age of AI*. Harvard Business Review Press

Drury, C. (2015), *Management and Cost Accounting* (9th edn). Cengage Learning

Forrester Research; Accenture Interactive (2016), *Expectations Vs. Experience: The Good, the Bad, the Opportunity*. Forrester Research

Freeman, J. (2009), Carrot Unstuck. *Boston Globe*, 8 March

Frye, A. and Campbell, D. (2011), Buffett Says Pricing Power More Important Than Good Management. *Bloomberg*, 18 February

Guthrie, J. (2018), How and When Zero-Based Budgeting Boosts Corporate Productivity. *Financial Times*, 21 February

Healy, G. (2016), *Bending the Cost Curve*. Accenture Strategy

Honts, R., Levesque, J. and Salvador, T. (2018), *The Front Office: Where Profits Go to Die*. Accenture Strategy

Hope, J. and Fraser, R. (2003), Who Needs Budgets? *Harvard Business Review*, February

IBM Corporation (2009), *Best-Practice Budgeting*. IBM Corporation

Kaplan, R. S. (2004), *Variance Analysis and Flexible Budgeting*. Harvard Business School Publishing

Kübler-Ross, E. and Kessler, D. (2005), *On Grief and Grieving: Finding the Meaning of Grief Through the Five Stages of Loss*. Simon & Schuster

Lake, M. (2018), How Zero-Based Principles Can Align Your Organization Around the Tech Capabilities That Matter. *CIO*, 21 August

Long, J., Roark, C. and Theofilou, B. (2018), *The Bottom Line on Trust: Achieve Competitive Agility*. Accenture Strategy

Marketing Interactive (2017), Unilever to Restructure and Slash Ad Spend. www.marketing-interactive.com/unilever-to-restructure-and-slash-ad-spend/

Mikells, K. (2017), Delivering Cultural Change to Fuel Our Growth. www.diageo.com/en/news-and-media/features/delivering-cultural-change-to-fuel-our-growth/

Nassauer, S. and Hufford, A. (2017), Wal-Mart Plans Further Cost Cuts as Competition with Amazon Intensifies. *Wall Street Journal*, 10 October

Needy, K. L. and Sarnowski, K. L. (2004), Keeping the Lid on Project Costs. In D. I. Cleland (ed.), *Field Guide to Project Management*, John Wiley and Sons, pp. 143–58

Nike (2012), NIKE Unveils Track & Field Footwear and Apparel Innovations. https://news.nike.com/news/track-field-nike-pro-turbospeed-uniforms-and-nike-zoom-spikes

OECD (2019), Gross Domestic Product (GDP): GDP, Volume – Annual Growth Rates in Percentage. https://stats.oecd.org/index.aspx?queryid=60703

Papa, T., Kaufman, A. and Maxwell, C. (2017), *When Bots Do the Buying: Procurement at 1/2 the Cost*. Accenture Strategy

Pearson, M. and Theofilou, B. (2017), *Formula Won: A New Way to Measure Corporate Competitiveness*. Accenture Strategy

Perez, A. (2018), *Quartile Zero: A New Way of Zero-Based Thinking*. Accenture Strategy

Pyhrr, P. (1970), Zero-Based Budgeting. *Harvard Business Review*, November–December

———(1973), *Zero-Base Budgeting: A Practical Management Tool for Evaluating Expenses*. John Wiley and Sons

Powell, C. (2018), *Unleashing the Future of Digital Finance*. Accenture Strategy

Pritchard, C. L. (2004), Why Project Management? In D. I. Cleland (ed.), *Field Guide to Project Management*, John Wiley and Sons, pp. 28–41

Prodhan, G. and Taylor, E. (2017), Adidas Partners with Siemens to Tailor Sporting Goods. *Reuters*, 24 April

Provost, L. P. and Langley, G. J. (1998), The Importance of Concepts in Creativity and Improvement. *Quality Progress*, March

Puricelli, S. J. (2016), What is S&OP? By Accenture Strategy Guest Blogger. https://blog.kinaxis.com/2016/06/sop-accenture-strategy-guest-blogger/

Salesforce (2018), Coca-Cola Germany. http://salesforce.vidyard.com/watch/BWJN4uT8voWR8LBf87uQ17?

Sight Machine (2016), *Jump Capital, GE Ventures and Two Roads Join $13.5 Million Series B Investment in Sight Machine*. San Francisco: Sight Machine

References

Steger, T., Barzey, C. and Viniak, V. (2018), *Time to Zero Base Your Telecom Business.* Accenture Strategy

The Coca-Cola Company (2014), The Coca-Cola Company Announces Actions to Drive Stronger Growth. www.coca-colacompany.com/press-center/press-releases/the-coca-cola-company-announces-actions-to-drive-stronger-growth

The Economist Intelligence Unit (2015), *Evidence-Based HR: The Bridge Between Your People and Delivering Business Strategy.* KPMG International Cooperative

Timmermans, K. (2015a), *Getting Ahead by Cutting Back: Using Zero-Based Budgeting to Fuel Growth.* Accenture

———(2015b), Zero-Based Budgeting: No Longer Just a Crisis Tool. *CFO,* 28 August

Timmermans, K. and Abdalla, R. (2018), *Beyond the ZBB Buzz.* Accenture

Timmermans, K. and Shuda, S. (2018), *Getting Ahead by Cutting Back.* Accenture Strategy

Trentmann, N. (2017), European Companies Use Old-School Budget Tactic to Cut Costs. *Wall Street Journal,* 7 April

———(2018), Global Companies Extend Use of Zero-Based Budgeting to Slash Costs. *Wall Street Journal,* 27 February

Unilever (2017), Accelerating Sustainable Shareholder Value Creation. www.unilever.com/news/press-releases/2017/Accelerating-sustainable-shareholder-value-creation.html

———(2018a), Good All-Round Performance with Accelerated Value Creation. www.unilever.com/news/press-releases/2018/good-all-round-performance-with-accelerated-value-creation.html

———(2018b), Unilever's Sustainable Living Plan Continues to Fuel Growth. www.unilever.com/news/press-releases/2018/unilevers-sustainable-living-plan-continues-to-fuel-growth.html

Valor Economico (2015), In AB Inbev, the Cost Reduction Never Ends. www.datamark.com.br/en/news/2015/5/in-ab-inbev-the-cost-reduction-never-ends-172675/

Wainewright, P. (2017), Salesforce Captures the Limits of AI in a Coca-Cola Cooler. *Diginomica,* 7 March

Acknowledgements

This book is built upon decades of dedicated client work from the excellent professionals at Accenture. Our gratitude goes out to them and to our colleagues who contributed by providing interviews and source materials: Kristen Andrews, Andrew Corr, Roger Ellison, Paul Jeruchimowitz, Alexis Perez, Amaury Reychler, Kristine Renker, Aaron Shifrin, Shin Shuda, Erika Simpson, Bill Theofilou, Jonathan Wicksall and Robert Willems. Lastly, we'd like to thank Mark Knickrehm, Group Chief Executive of Accenture Strategy, for his support from day one of this project.

We owe a debt of gratitude to Jean Ostvoll, Executive Director, Marketing and Communications, Accenture Strategy, who steered the creation of this book so adroitly. You challenged us, pushed us out of our comfort zones, and elevated our work. Jenn Glatt, thank you for running a tight ship in the early stages of manuscript development. Catherine Pettersson, kudos for managing to knit poetry throughout our prose. To Miriam Mehrkens, thanks for dotting our i's and crossing our t's.

Finally, thanks to the intrepid team at Penguin: Martina O'Sullivan, Emma Brown and Trevor Horwood.

Glossary

A rock and a hard place The expression 'between a rock and a hard place' supposedly comes from Homer's *Odyssey*, when Odysseus has to sail between two rocky islands, choosing his path between Scylla (a six-headed monster living in the rock) and Charybdis (a deadly whirlpool – the hard place).

Algorithm A list of rules to be followed in order to solve a problem. Because any given task can be accomplished in many different ways – i.e. by using one or more of many different algorithms – and each of them has advantages and disadvantages in different situations, it's key to know the strengths and weaknesses of each when applied to the task at hand before deciding which to use.

BI Business Intelligence. The business intelligence evolution is trending toward increased autonomy and advanced data visualization. Organizations want much more from their analytics solutions than simply a single version of the truth to drive effective decision making or meet reporting requirements. They want easy, fast, intuitive access to both structured and unstructured data. In real time. At their fingertips. Whenever and wherever.

CAPEX Capital expenditures. The resources used to create future benefit, such as the purchase of capital goods or services that will be used for more than one year – fixed assets, for example. When the asset begins to be used, it's amortized over time to spread the tax-deductible cost over its useful life. Companies usually budget for CAPEX purchases separately from the operational budget.

Carrot and stick An incentive system in which people are rewarded for some behaviours and threatened with punishment for others. The 'carrot and stick' phrase allegedly dates to an 1876 review of a book on John Stuart Mill, referring to the 'carrot and stick discipline' to which his father subjected him.[1]

Change concepts A change concept is a general notion or approach to develop specific ideas for changes that lead to improvement, including many that do not require trade-offs between costs and quality. Change concepts usually provoke new ways of thinking about the problem or opportunity at hand.[2]

Closed-loop management Accenture's closed-loop cost management approach provides deep visibility on all expenses – across business units, categories and geographies – to identify, eliminate and prevent unproductive spend on an ongoing basis. It's a six-step methodology – visibility, value targeting, category ownership, locking targets into budgets, execution of initiatives, and control and monitoring – to help drive sustainable cost reduction.

COGS Cost of goods sold. Refers to the direct costs incurred in the production of the goods sold by a company, including those of materials and direct labour.

Competitive agility To be competitive in today's environment, companies need to execute a balanced strategy that simultaneously prioritizes growth, profitability, sustainability and trust. The Accenture Strategy Competitive Agility Index scores more than 7,000 companies across these three interdependent dimensions of competitiveness.

Cost-to-serve The total cost of serving your customers at a certain product/service level, according to the specific actual business activities and corresponding overhead costs incurred.

CRM Customer relationship management.

C-suite A company's executive employees, such as chief executive officer (CEO), chief financial officer (CFO), chief operating officer (COO), and chief information officer (CIO).

EBITDA Earnings before interest, tax, depreciation and amortization.

EPM Enterprise performance management.

ERP Enterprise resource planning.

Five stages of grief The five stages of grief – denial, anger, bargaining, depression and acceptance – are a part of the framework that makes up our learning to live with bereavement. But not everyone goes through all of them or goes through them in a prescribed order. They are responses to loss that many people have, but there is not a typical response to loss, as there is no typical loss. Our grief is as individual as our lives.[3]

Force majeure A French term that translates literally as 'superior force' and refers to the occurrence of events that cannot be anticipated or are beyond one's control, such as war, strikes, riots or 'acts of God' such as hurricane, flood, earthquake, volcanic eruption, etc.

FTE Full-time equivalent. An FTE of 1.0 indicates a requirement for one full-time person, while smaller numbers reflect part-time requirements.

G&A General and administrative costs.

GIS Geographic information system. A technology used for spatial asset management. GIS is fundamental in automation, sensors and the integration of information technology and operational technology. It enables the exchange of data between GIS, operations and enterprise resource planning systems.[4]

Hardwire To cause a pattern of behaviour or certain mental processes to become automatic, standard, or instinctive.

IIoT Industrial internet of things. A universe of intelligent products, processes and services that communicate with each other and with people over the internet. It has been heralded primarily as a way to improve operational efficiency, but in the future successful companies will use IIoT to capture new growth through three approaches: boosting revenues by increasing production and creating new hybrid business models; exploiting intelligent technologies to fuel innovation; and transforming their workforce.[5]

KPI Key performance indicator.

Non-working money Expenses incurred independently from sales volumes or revenues and without immediate benefit to consumers.

OECD Organisation for Economic Co-operation and Development, an international organization with thirty-six member countries including not only many of the world's most advanced nations from North America, Europe and Asia-Pacific but also emerging ones such as Mexico, Chile and Turkey.

OEE Overall equipment effectiveness.

OPEX Operating expenditures. The resources used to run day-to-day business operations. Unlike CAPEX, operating expenses are fully tax-deductible in the year they are spent.

OTC Order-to-cash. A set of business processes that ranges from capturing and fulfilling customer requests for goods or services to receiving the corresponding payment.

OTIF One-time installation fee.

P&L Profit and loss.

Product or service costing The process of calculating the cost of each product or service, usually by adding the direct costs plus a contribution towards the overheads of the business.

Quartile A statistical term describing a split of observations from a specific range of data into four intervals, each with an equal number of observations.

ROI Return on investment. A performance ratio used to analyse the efficiency of a specific investment or compare the efficiency of a group of different investment options. ROI directly measures the return on a particular investment (the net profit) in relation to that investment's cost.

RPA Robotic process automation. A technology that emulates and automates tasks performed by humans. RPA provides companies with a virtual workforce that is set up to connect with their systems in the front office, back office and support functions in the same way as existing users. This technology often adds the most value for companies with manual, high-volume, repetitive, rule-based processes involving structured data, such as transaction processing. For this reason, financial services have seen higher rates of adoption than other industries.

S&OP Sales and operations planning. An operating model to help organizations make better business decisions when trying to match supply and demand and balancing the cost (supply) and service (demand) trade-offs of the supply chain.[6]

S/4HANA An ERP software package developed by the software corporation SAP SE.

Seat charge The costs associated with the use of a physical location by an employee, which usually include facilities (real estate and utilities), IT spend and any overhead associated with the maintenance of the seat.

SG&A Selling, general and administrative expenses. All non-production expenses incurred by a company in any given period.

SKU Stock-keeping unit. A unique type of item (product or service) with specific attributes that distinguish it from the others, such as supplier, material, size, colour, packaging, etc.

TMS Transportation management system.

VA Virtual assistant.

VRO Value-realization office.

Working money Expenses with a direct impact on sales volumes or revenues.

YTD Year to date.

ZBB Zero-based budgeting.

ZBC Zero-based commercial.

ZBO Zero-based organization.

ZBS Zero-based spend.

ZBSC Zero-based supply chain.

ZBx Zero-based mindset. More holistic than zero-based budgeting, ZBx is a new zero-based mindset and a holistic approach to help you identify non-working money to reinvest and so ignite your growth strategy and foster competitive agility.

Notes

Introduction: A Rock and a Hard Place

1. Accenture (2015a).
2. OECD (2019).
3. Accenture (2015b).
4. Pearson and Theofilou (2017).
5. Long, Roark and Theofilou (2018).
6. Unilever (2018a).
7. Unilever (2017).
8. Trentmann (2017).
9. Unilever (2018b).

1. The (R)evolution of ZBx

1. Valor Economico (2015).
2. The Coca-Cola Company (2014).
3. ConAgra Foods, Inc. (2015).
4. Mikells (2017).
5. Marketing Interactive (2017).
6. Nassauer and Hufford (2017).
7. Trentmann (2018).
8. Pyhrr (1970).
9. Pyhrr (1973).
10. Daneshkhu, Whipp and Fontanella-Khan (2017).
11. Correa (2014).
12. Guthrie (2018).
13. Timmermans and Abdalla (2018).

14. Perez (2018).

15. Daugherty and Wilson (2018).

2. The 'X' Factor

1. Accenture Strategy (2016a).

2. Timmermans and Shuda (2018).

3. Barea, Banerjee, Feliciano and Mueller (2017).

4. Corr (2018).

5. Unilever (2018a).

6. Corr (2018).

7. Ibid.

8. Steger, Barzey and Viniak (2018).

3. Zeroing in on Cost Curves

1. Daugherty and Wilson (2018).

2. Perez (2018).

3. Daugherty and Wilson (2018).

4. Babcock (2016).

5. Sight Machine (2016).

6. Daugherty and Wilson (2018).

7. Salesforce (2018).

8. Wainewright (2017).

9. Daugherty and Wilson (2018).

10. Lake (2018).

11. Prodhan and Taylor (2017).

12. Corr (2018).

13. Nike (2012).

14. Bhatt (2018).

15. Healy (2016).

16. Accenture Strategy (2017).

17. Forrester Research; Accenture Interactive (2016).

18. Papa, Kaufman and Maxwell (2017).
19. Accenture (2016b).
20. Lake (2018).
21. Perez (2018).

4. 'The way we should do things around here'

1. Timmermans (2015b).
2. Andrews (2018).
3. Barea, Banerjee, Feliciano and Mueller (2017).
4. Ibid.
5. Accenture Strategy (2016b).

5. A Taste of the Secret Sauce

1. Timmermans and Abdalla (2018).

6. Driving Visibility – Moving from Denial to Acceptance

1. Kübler-Ross and Kessler (2005).
2. Timmermans and Abdalla (2018).
3. Accenture (2015b).
4. Needy and Sarnowski (2004).
5. Drury (2015).
6. Askew (2016).
7. The Economist Intelligence Unit (2015).
8. Timmermans (2015a).
9. Timmermans and Abdalla (2018).
10. Needy and Sarnowski (2004).

7. *Value Targeting – Nailing the Ambition*

1. Provost and Langley (1998).
2. Frye and Campbell (2011).
3. Honts, Levesque and Salvador (2018).

8. *Category Ownership – Shining Light in the Darkest Corners*

1. Timmermans (2015a).

9. *Lock Targets into the Budget – Promises, Promises*

1. IBM Corporation (2009).
2. Ibid.

10. *Execute Initiatives – from Theory to Action*

1. Timmermans (2015b).
2. Accenture client experience.
3. Honts, Levesque and Salvador (2018).
4. Accenture client experience.
5. Pritchard (2004).

11. *Control and Monitoring – Racing Ahead*

1. Kaplan (2004).
2. Ibid.
3. Hope and Fraser (2003).

4. Kaplan (2004).
5. Powell (2018).

Parting thoughts . . .

1. Timmermans and Abdalla (2018).
2. Timmermans (2015b).

Glossary

1. Freeman (2009).
2. Provost and Langley (1998).
3. Kübler-Ross and Kessler (2005).
4. Accenture (2016a).
5. Daugherty, Banerjee, Negm and Alter (2015).
6. Puricelli (2016).

About Accenture

Accenture is a leading global professional services company, providing a broad range of services and solutions in strategy, consulting, digital, technology and operations. Combining unmatched experience and specialized skills across more than forty industries and all business functions – underpinned by the world's largest delivery network – Accenture works at the intersection of business and technology to help clients improve their performance and create sustainable value for their stakeholders. With 469,000 people serving clients in more than 120 countries, Accenture drives innovation to improve the way the world works and lives. Visit us at www.accenture.com.

Accenture Strategy combines deep industry expertise, advanced analytics capabilities and human-led design methodologies that enable clients to act with speed and confidence. By identifying clear, actionable paths to accelerate competitive agility, Accenture Strategy helps leaders in the C-suite envision and execute strategies that drive growth in the face of digital transformation. For more information, follow @AccentureStrat or visit www.accenture.com/strategy.